FOUR   FIELDS—FIVE   GATES

Four Fields, Five Gate

FOUR FIELDS
FIVE GATES

By
ANNE LORIS HILL

JOHN JONES

ɪ ᴏa.   *ᴇs*
by
Anne L. Hill

first published in 1954 by Herbert Jenkins, London

This edition © John Jones Publishing Ltd
published March 1999

ISBN 1 871083 71 0

Printed by
Gwasg Dinefwr Press, Llandybie, Carmarthenshire

Published by
John Jones Publishing Ltd., Clwydfro Business Centre,
Ruthin, North Wales, LL15 1NJ

To MAT

To remind her, when old age comes
of what we once did.

LIST OF ILLUSTRATIONS

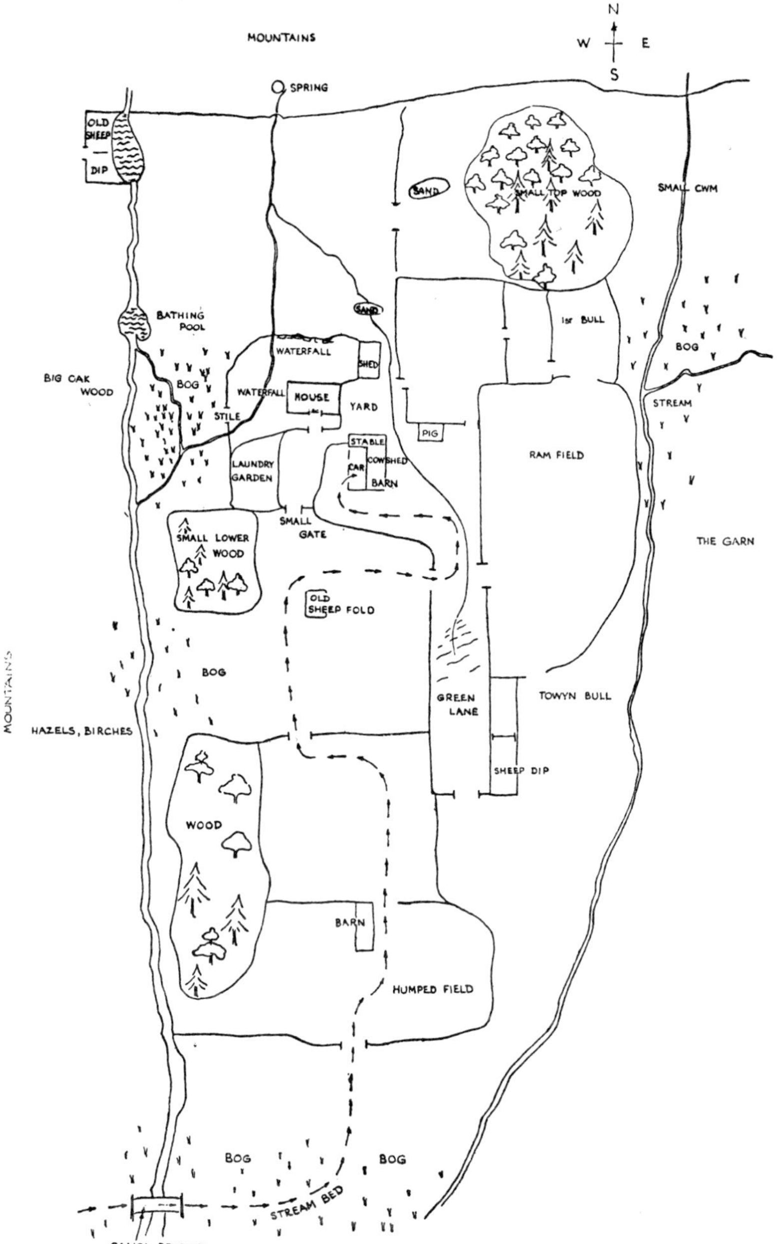

MOUNTAINS
N
W
E
S
SPRING
OLD SHEEP DIP
SAND
SMALL TOP WOOD
SMALL CWM
SAND
1st BULL
BATHING POOL
WATERFALL
SHED
BOG
BIG OAK WOOD
BOG
WATERFALL
HOUSE
YARD
STILE
STREAM
PIG
STABLE
CAR
COWSHED
BARN
LAUNDRY GARDEN
RAM FIELD
SMALL GATE
SMALL LOWER WOOD
THE GARN
OLD SHEEP FOLD
MOUNTAINS
BOG
GREEN LANE
TOWYN BULL
HAZELS, BIRCHES
SHEEP DIP
WOOD
BARN
HUMPED FIELD
BOG
BOG
STREAM BED
CANOL BRIDGE

CHAPTER I

WE had left Wales early in the morning and reached home soon after dusk. Walking down the small flagged path, I took the key from under the stone by the step and turned it in the lock. As I pushed open the door, it rustled over the orange envelope of a telegram. Its message read, " Strongly recommend delightful old farmhouse in this valley letter following Kath ".

We had been looking for a house for a long time—so long that I cannot remember clearly in what year the search began. I can only recall that it finished in 1940.

The search was not for a house with as many " Modern Conveniences " as we could pay for, and from which we could get to work as easily as possible each day. We already had that. Fate, in its inscrutable fashion, had given us jobs in a flat and populous county, and we, in the contrary manner of human beings, longing for hills, had come to the conclusion that we must find a house in Wales, where we could forget, in holidays, the level and limited horizon bounding our daily view.

Our demands had not been high : if we could find a place sufficiently remote and in beautiful enough surroundings, we were prepared to overlook all minor drawbacks, provided the walls went all the way round, and the roof was more or less sound.

We had seen enough of Wales to make us quite sure that the house must be somewhere on the northern slopes of the Mawddach estuary above the 400-foot contour, between Dolgelley and the sea. We searched high, for anything nearer sea-level would almost certainly be occupied. In the mountains were derelict buildings of all kinds, often relics of the period when slate quarries, gold and manganese mines were productive, but now, most of them were dilapidated beyond rescue. They stood—mere ruined walls—for doors and windows had long since disappeared, and the dark openings stared into the mountains with sightless eyes. Tall rank nettles grew around them, and the paths to their doors, through disuse, were narrow as rabbit tracks. The years had slowly gathered piles of broken slates at the foot of their walls, torn from the roof by gales, or through the sheer inability of their oak pegs to cling any longer to the rotting rafters. Other homesteads might be small farmhouses left by sheep farmers in the move towards greater prosperity in the lower valley, for in the mountains, greater prosperity always means a move to live further from them.

Wales has many of these houses, and most of them will never be occupied again. They are too isolated for modern life. I was always meeting someone who remembered living in one as a child, or whose father was born there. As economic circumstances improved, they moved nearer to civilization, or at any rate, nearer to a thicker population.

The small offshoots from the main track were most likely to provide what we sought, for the main track, poor as it might be, was a modern convenience of kinds ; mod. cons. are after all, comparative, and it was likely that any house with a usable track was inhabited.

We took with us a pair of binoculars because they saved us the walk to discover whether a building had a chimney, for a chimney indicated a house and not a barn. If it had one we looked for smoke. Very few of the small Welsh farms use oil for cooking, and never yet have we come across one with the fire out, so it was pretty certain that if a farm were inhabited, we should know it at a distance by its smoking chimney.

But in 1939, when war came, we evacuated our school from London, and after an incredibly weary day found ourselves in billets in a small Oxfordshire village. Here, for some months, we gave up all notions of a cottage in Wales, but found, as an escape from billets, an old cottage in the village, made new with electric light and a bath with taps, but no water beyond a well in our neighbour's garden, from which, as an act of courtesy, we were allowed to draw our not very hygienic water. In this cottage, Ruth, Mat and myself threw in our lots together and decided to live.

Mat and I dashed up to London one evening, and brought out our cars, hers an old Morris 8, mine an even older M.G., and they also were moved into a healthy fresh-air life in an open shed further up the village.

By the time Easter came we were well settled in and preparing once more for the search. The day after school closed Mat and I started for the Mawddach estuary to stay with Kath and Iolo, who, for years, had tenanted an old longhouse there. We left in the late afternoon, and at eleven o'clock on that cold, starry night we ground up their stony hill and parked the car under their larch tree—a bent and ancient tree that raises annually, in a hole in its lowest bough, a large brood of blue tits.

We talked drowsily over the fire in the soft light of the oil lamp and stumbled upstairs to our cruck-walled bedroom at two o'clock. When the candle was blown out I could distinguish Cader Idris across the valley through the small window, a bright star moving slowly across the sky above it. The night was clear and still ; its long silences broken only by the distant hoot of owls in the wood and the bleating of sheep on the mountain.

Kath's house, wherever she lives, has always been the nicest place to spend a holiday. You may rise at four in the morning—or not at all. You may come early or late for meals ; no one frowns. Suggestions of a day on Snowdon or Tryfan are eagerly taken up ; and if, as a result, one walks all day in rain, clothes are dried without fuss or bother. Hot water bottles are always hot : winter fires are blazing. Books line the walls, chairs are deep and old and comfortable, and you may fall asleep in one at any hour without comment. Life is leisurely ; there is time to stand and stare.

We explored the district thoroughly, and, as usual, we found nothing that would do.

" You could furnish our little barn," said Iolo, " until you find something better."

" Silly," said Kath, " it's got no windows or fireplace."

Iolo lives on a different mental plane from most people.

" Hasn't it ? " he said, in great surprise, " I must go and see." He returned with the air of one who has made a great discovery. "She's right," he said. "It hasn't," so that grateful as we were for the spirit in which the offer was made, we declined the substance.

The holiday ended and we returned, leaving on a morning when the frosted top of Cader was just touched by a pink sunrise, and driving through the daylight hours of a frosty spring day. Back in Oxfordshire, we found the telegram—sent a few hours after we had left.

We put the kettle on and pondered. Working on our usual theory of smoking chimneys being inhabited houses, we were quite certain that every house in that valley was occupied. Perhaps the house had been vacated that very day—or perhaps there was some hidden cwm, which, in the manner of the Gaelic legend, appeared only occasionally.

Next morning, Mat was up very early, an unusual occurrence, and waiting outside the village post office for our letters. Among them was Kath's.

The house, she said, was about seven hundred feet up and three miles from the estuary. The owner would let, provided we were willing to leave him one room for his own use, where he could boil a kettle and have a meal before he went the rounds of the sheep there. It lay in a small and secluded cwm. Iolo, walking to Diphwys with Kath after our departure, had nonchalantly waved his stick towards it as he said,

"What a long time the house down there has been empty!"

"Which house?" asked Kath, aghast, and seeing none.

"Down there, out of sight," said he.

As I have said before, Iolo lives in another world. Just occasionally, as here, it impinges on other people's worlds. Kath wasted no time in protests. In two hours they had found the owner. Blaen-cwm-Mynach (the name of which means "the head of the valley of the monks")—the house we were to take—was the farm on which he had lived from birth before he too, moved nearer to prosperity. To reach it one passed through four fields and five gates after leaving the main track. The roof leaked badly but he would repair it. In prolonged bad weather, the lower field flooded, but never too deeply to wade. Finally, the house had been empty for twenty years.

If it had waited twenty years, it seemed unnecessary to hurry, but I already imagined hordes of people, all intent on taking that particular house, pouring off the early train and starting up the valley to sign the lease. However, there was time. It was not nine o'clock yet and their train was far from Dolgelley. They would have to find the owner before they could do anything. The toll-bridge road was half a mile across, and they would probably miss the bus to Bontddu. They might even get lost. Kath would have time to be ahead of them all.

We wired " Please take it and pay a year's rent Mat and Anne."

After a long impatient period of waiting, in which the only highlight was the exchange of the M.G. for a Singer tourer, there came a Saturday in May when we decided we had saved enough petrol to make the trip to see the house, going and returning the same day if we started very early and took turns at driving.

On the previous night, we had gathered together the usual collection of articles for a longish run—pick, spade and chains in case our four fields were soft and muddy ; spirit kettle, sandwiches and a cache of miscellaneous articles, slowly amassed during the years of search. As dark fell, we loaded our nucleus of household goods into the car, leaving just enough room for Ruth to squeeze in beside. At ten o'clock we left the car in readiness with the dew sparkling on its hood in the moonlight.

Before dawn we were off. Accompanied by strange tinklings and rattlings of ironmongery and crockery, we climbed the hill from the village and careered joyfully along the roads running high across Oxfordshire in the bright, cool freshness of a May morning. As the sun rose, rooks flew from the high elms of the field sides, and on the verges, early thrushes tugged early worms from the dewy grass. We descended Fish Hill into Broadway, little rabbits scuttling across the road and disappearing through unseen holes in the hedge at our approach. Broadway itself was not awake ;

there was no one about in its main street and it looked much nicer than usual.

By mid-morning we were well into Wales and as we passed the old hawthorns near the hairpin bends of Bwlch-y-Fedwen, spring too seemed to have reached mid-Wales. There were small, green buds in the hedges and a soft benign look on the moors. A pile of peat was drying in the sun near the roadside. Mat, beside me, idly playing a Tipperary flute, put it down to say,

"We shan't need to spend anything on coal. We can cut tons and tons of peat."

Reaching the top of the Dinas Mawddwy pass, we started on the long swinging slope to Cross Foxes. The east face of Cader rose before us, little wisps of cloud floating across the front of it, and below and beyond, dim suggestions of the Mawddach estuary in misty sun. Through the turns and twists of the wooded road we reached Dolgelley, left the narrow streets, crossed the river, drove on to the foot of our valley, and climbed upwards.

Water was tumbling in a glorious cascade under the first stone bridge. I watched from the cramped back seat while Ruth opened the gate. Pussy willows bloomed along the edge of the stream, and the bog-myrtle was putting out its vivid red-brown catkins. Beyond the next bridge, its low walls covered in map-lichens and tiny wire-stemmed ferns springing from the old mortar, we came in sight of the farm-house where we were to meet our landlord. On the sunny slopes gorse was bursting into yellow sprays. Beneath the bridge the water rushed through little brown pools under leaning, black-catkinned alders, and disappeared suddenly round a bend into the bog. A wood of oaks, tall and straggly, stretched to the light, each trying to outgrow its neigh-bour. Near the horizon, the great, grey slabs of the mountain lay on their backs looking at the brilliant blue sky. The air was warm and still, and the sun shone on myriads of insects flitting in whorls and circles over the water. The happy feeling of one's first spring day came over me.

Below the house, we stopped, and a horde of what seemed

like twenty fierce dogs rushed at us as we set foot out of the car. My first reaction was to get back quickly, but realization that the dogs were to be our near neighbours brought a change of mind ; they must be made to understand by our unyielding front that we were not afraid of them. Since I was, it was hard to appear unconcerned.

A more pressing incident however, sent us all scrambling back. A square-headed, black Welsh bull was stepping towards us very deliberately through the bog myrtle. It seemed a forlorn hope to present a united front here. I wished I'd got a car with four doors instead of two, for I was front passenger now, and last in. Mat, who was driving, shot off while I was only half inside, my feet trailing over the running-board. Well out of sight of the creature we stopped again and got out. The twenty dogs had cantered along with us, making savage leaps as we peered out of the back window, bullwards. The house door opened, and as two figures emerged, a stream of Welsh words was hurled at the dogs, who, rather unwillingly, ceased their racket and fell back, circling us suspiciously as though we were part of a recalcitrant flock. Many noses were pushed uncomfortably near my calves as we moved towards the house, and I determined that one of my first personal purchases would be a pair of tough Wellingtons.

The two men came to meet us ; Richard Jones, our landlord, and Willie, his son, who lived here with his sister Enid and helped his father to farm this and the land of Blaen-y-cwm which marched with it. Richard Jones was wiry and rosy-faced, with far-seeing, bright, blue eyes ; Willie was very like him. We shook hands and I remarked on what was uppermost in our minds.

" Ah, yes," said Richard Jones, " we let him out on fine days at this time of year to work off his fierceness."

I hoped it would have worn off by our next visit.

" But he will not be here in the summer. We shall keep him in Blaen-y-cwm."

The Welsh idiom caused me a passing uneasiness—not, I thought, surely, in the room where the kettle was to be boiled ? He went on,

"Many people go by in the summer to climb the mountains, and he will be safer away in the little cwm."

I wondered—safer for whom?

He came with us to the car, and pointed to the north.

"You can see from here the stone wall running down the mountain to the wood. There you will find the house."

I looked. Just visible above leafless branches about a mile away rose one chimney of Blaen-y-cwm.

"I think the bridge will be wide enough for your car, but," he added, dubiously, "you must be careful—no car has ever crossed it." He handed to us a great rusty key about six inches long, and we started in the direction of the chimney while he followed on foot. The milder-mannered of the dogs accompanied him, but one, a Thurber-like animal resembling a shaggy hearthrug, stayed behind. I was relieved to see this out of the corner of my eye, for he had led the pack and started the hullabaloo.

Driving along a narrow, stone-walled lane, overgrown with short, vivid green grass, we were soon on the mountain itself. Beside the track, from between two rocks shaped oddly like a flower pot, grew a little conifer looking like a Christmas tree. We went very slowly, often not even in gear, but just rolling down one incline and lurching up the next in an attempt to avert the larger and more sickening thuds of our heavy load on to the springs.

As the way petered out we turned by an old and empty farmhouse. The view from here was very beautiful—a foreground of low, uneven walls and turfed lane running to a little enclosure and down to a pool where the stream widened. At the other side, the greens, browns and russets of bog were broken by white tufts of cotton grass and brilliant pincushions of emerald moss, and cut by the black, peaty ditches. Behind, the colours darkened to a broad band of oak wood, not yet in leaf, and the sharply-lined tree-tops rose, rank upon rank, an occasional holly or ivy-grown mass adding a sun-touched green. Still higher, the grey rocks of the Garn lay at all angles, their deep clefts thrown into dark, grotesque shadows; and towards the summit, the sage-green turf swept up and met the sky.

We arrived at the bridge—not yet crossed by a car—and I hoped fervently that mine was not to be the sacrificial one. The bridge was made of great lengths of stone laid on rough stone piers, built dry-walled in the stream. There were no side-walls to hem one in, and give, at any rate the illusion of security. The bridge was short, so that if we dropped through, one pair of wheels might remain on land, and it was low, so that if it gave way, we should not be impossible to salvage. It was a rough, rude structure, attractive to look upon. But, casual though it looked, I realize now, after seeing the floods that rise and batter it, that great skill had gone to its making ; an old, inherited skill, so old as to have become unconscious in its makers·

A few lurches, a few rushes, a few rollings back, and we were over. This side of the stream was Blaen-y-cwm land, and was little but bog, stream and boulders. I splashed on alone up the watercourse, while Mat and Ruth followed on foot for the sake of the car. Greenish yellow stars of butter-wort grew along the sides, and the red-browns of bog asphodel brightened the fringes of the pools.

Turning into the last field, I suddenly looked up and saw the house looking down the slope towards me. It stood on a little rise with the mountains behind it, shepherded into place by the surrounding slopes ; oblong, solid and unpre-tentious, its door in the middle, a window on each side, with upstairs, symmetrically placed, the three smaller windows of the bedrooms. New patches of lime shone on the roof where holes had been repaired, and a huge chimney sur-mounted each end. The sun shone full on its face from the south, and gave it a peaceful, placid air. It looked entirely right in its surroundings. Built from the stone which lay just beyond its walls, it was impossible it should be otherwise. I stood and looked at it, my heart beating quickly with pleasure, and the house stood and looked sleepily back at me, almost nodding its head and saying,

" Yes, I've waited a long time—twenty years, winter and summer—twenty years."

I sat on a rock there, looking, until the others came up, and as they reached the sheepfold, I saw from Mat's expres-sion, that it was the right house for her, too.

In the front door, the church-door-like key fitted upside down and turned the wrong way. A key at all was super-fluous, for the timber was rotten, its surface stabbed with the minute burrows of woodworm, which were slowly turning it to powder. The hinges gave out deep, agonized groans as the door fell back. It opened straight into the hall, spacious and dignified, with a ceiling beamed and white-washed. Thick cobwebs wavered from each beam, catching the sun as they floated out in draughts from the open door. The sun too, cast bright narrow oblongs through the panes above on to the floor, which was of large, uneven, stone slabs, worn down at the corners where contact with many boots had chipped away the layers. From the right the stairs led—wide, shallow steps of oak, with an unornamented stair rail, worn smooth from the touch of many hands.

The big kitchen on the left had a plank door with rusty strap-hinges. The hearth was perhaps eight feet wide, with a great black beam above it, and a small rusted iron door in a side recess covered the bread oven. The high window, almost opaque with dust, looked on to an old holly tree just outside. I rubbed a small clear space on the glass, and saw down the slope the view on which the house had grown placid, the little gate leading to the tiny fields and sheep-folds, the barn roof in the humped field, the rugged moun-tains sloping down at each side of the valley, and away at the bottom, the rise of foothills to the long sweep of Cader itself.

The kitchen floor was slabbed like the hall. But what slabs! Erected vertically, they would have made as good a practice climbing-ground as any in Snowdonia. Not one lay at the same angle; no two were worn in the same place.

Long shreds of wallpaper hung from the dryer walls; from the wet ones, all paper had long since disappeared, and the only decoration was an uneven fringe of dark green moss, growing sometimes at the base, in other places just below ceiling height. Fortunately, the walls beneath seemed sound and well plastered. Fungus, looking sickly from lack of light, pushed through in dark corners. Opposite the window a long deal dresser ran almost the width of the room. Its heavy drawers needed both hands to wrench them open, so swollen were they with the damp.

We went along the hall and through the door at the back. Here, the building was one-storyed. There were three rooms, separated by unplastered, whitewashed stone walls. Facing west was the dairy, its floor red-tiled ; a steep oak wood filled the window view. The iron gears and shafts from the water-wheel outside—once used for churning—projected through the wall, and were anchored solidly to a great beam a couple of feet from the floor. The nuts securing it were shaled away, and the once square-headed bolts had become a nondescript shape. The middle place was small and dark with a tiny window, whose sill was lower than the bank on to which it looked. Rushes and foxgloves swayed outside in the breeze against a background of mountain and sky, making the window appear like a small, framed and lovely picture.

The remaining room was the same size as the dairy and faced over the yard to the small cwm (where the bull was to live), and up to the terraces of Y Garn. The walls of these back rooms were roughly built—very little better than a good barn, and not much mortar had been wasted on them. Breezes made entry through scores of ways between the stones, and there was a constant circulation of air even on that mild, Spring day. Above the dairy window, the oak-pegged slates were visible where the plaster had left the laths. I poked the lower part of the roof tentatively, and a slate slowly slipped and grated over its next neighbour as it slid towards the bank.

In the hall, a dark cupboard beneath the stairs held a few dusty pieces of coal, and volumes of damp-smelling, stagnant air.

Upstairs, directly over the hall, was a small bedroom, with a large one on each side. These two looked immense. One of them would have taken six single beds with ease. Irregular patches on the walls were green with moss like those of the kitchen. From the side of the window I scooped a small cushion of it, with pale brown seed-heads, large enough to put in a rock-garden, and fungus of a different species from that in the kitchen grew in one corner.

We went downstairs and into the open air, walking round the house walls to see whether collapse was imminent, but were reassured to find the shell of the house was thick and strong. It was built of roughly-shaped blocks of stone and looked sound enough except for the lack of mortar. The back roof had the gentle undulation which comes from age, and was tiled with rough, hand-cut slates. Looking into the deep gulley at the base of the back walls, Mat said cheerfully,

"Lots of slates about for repair work." There were of course—those that had slid off. The south-facing wall was in the best condition, and the angle at which the old trees leant showed that it was from the south that the storms beat up the valley.

We returned to the bedrooms and I sat in a window looking down the valley and thinking that we could have found no better situation and view if the search had gone on for ever, and as for the house, our minimum demand had been for a strong, stone shell. We had more. It had interior walls, doors, ceilings, wooden-floored bedrooms, and, what we could never have hoped for—oak stairs.

High above the little fields a pair of ravens were swooping on a buzzard. Many times since have I watched them sparring together there. In the first field a group of black calves stood in a motionless circle, looking curiously at the car, and on all the outcrops of rock, lambs played idiotically in the May sunshine.

Beyond them, Richard Jones was approaching the last slope and we went down to meet him. It was very obvious as he talked, that he loved this place of his birth and found pleasure in feeling that it was to be inhabited again, and by people who, in time, might feel as he did about it. As holiday has followed holiday we have come to know him better, and now rarely a week passes when he fails to call in on one of his rounds to have a cup of tea with us before he starts back over the mountain for home. At sunset, when we have talked of sheep and foxes, the bilberry crop prospects, the gulls' nests and the ducks on the lake, and the behaviour of the tractor, he stands up and looks out of the window, saying,

"What is the time? I must be starting before night catches me on the old mountain." We have grown very fond of him.

His kettle-boiling room was opposite to the kitchen. A huge, worn old table occupied most of the space. Round it were one or two strong, country-made chairs and a pair of shearing benches. Old plates and cups, with faded, washed-away patterns, rested on a plate-rack fastened to the wall, and shining shears in their leather cases were on the window-sill. Bottles of Cooper's Dip, castor oil, turpentine and sheep-marking fluid filled a shelf near the fireplace. Rusty nails, files, bits of old chain, marking-irons and a packet of salt turned almost to liquid in the damp, lay on a small, round, three-legged table. Rolled up on the floor were a couple of fleeces and an armful of heather and birch twigs lay drying, for the next kettle-boiling. Looking sternly at each other from opposite walls, were sombre-coloured plates of Gladstone and Disraeli.

We went outside again and up the hollowed stone steps to the stable-loft, where the last clip of wool lay waiting to be fetched away to the mills. Underneath were the cattle stalls, and a corrugated-iron roof at one side, supported on oak trunks, made a lean-to, as a rough shelter for the old mowing-machine with its home-made shaft, and for more shearing benches of thick slabs of wood with four sturdy legs of oak stakes set in, splayed, at each corner.

Across the yard and nearer the mountain were the empty pig sties. If pigs be conscious of their surroundings, then the Blaen-y-cwm pigs must have been the most æsthetic of their race. The terraces of the Garn swept down almost to their walls. Cumulus towered in great cauliflower shapes in the sky, and waterfalls ran in creased white ribbons down the rocks. Long walls laboured up and down across the grey face, broken in places where precipitous cliffs made their construction unnecessary or impossible.

The house and buildings stood on about an acre of green turf snatched from the mountains and bog surrounding them, and were enclosed by low walls of boulders, cast around like protecting arms, to keep the mountain from reclaiming its own again. Tall bracken grew above the walls on the outside and gazed hungrily over. Where, through age and weather, the walls had fallen, bracken was stealthily creeping in through the gaps on to the smooth turf.

Perhaps in that time twenty years ago, this had been the garden. Now, it was just short, green mountain turf grazed by the sheep, which walked familiarly in through the gaps, or leapt the low walls. At the bottom was the little gate conducting the barely seen footpath to the place where I had left the car, a short cut for foot passengers, for the track itself still had two more gates and a lane before it curved into the yard. On the west, was a smaller, sunken piece of ground lying cheek by jowl with a tiny, boulder-strewn wood. Where it met the mountain, the wall was supported by grotesque, wind-battered blackthorn bushes, their twigs trailing with long, streaming grey moss, like matted hair. A narrow stile dropped down to the bog, where a track such as Llewellyn might have known wound through the drier parts.

From the mountain, a narrow stream tore a gully through the peat and seethed its way under the wall. Lower down stood the water-wheel, stilled for many a year. Rusty nails projected from the rotten slats ready to fall out after another winter. In past days, when the water was in spate and the gears harnessed, the dairy must have rocked like a windmill. The stream fell over a worn stone trough into a small pool, and then, suddenly shy, crept to the bog, gurgling away in a hollow voice beneath boulders, and hiding itself under cover of spreading clumps of rushes. The bog itself was alive with streams and behind them, the oaks seen from the dairy window rose to the lake track.

It was hard to think. The search had taken so long that it was difficult to realize it had ended.

We drove the car up the last bit of rackety track and unloaded it, stacking everything in the middle of the dormitory floor, like a base camp established in an unexplored waste.

The afternoon was gone. Richard Jones started over Mynydd Mynach for home. The evening sun had left the valley before we were ready to go, but the tops of the west-facing mountains were still touched with a golden light, which crept higher as we watched, then fled to the tops and vanished. A cold, dark look was on the water as we rocked over the bridge again, and the young birches were a rich purple-brown in the dusk. The air was chilly and clear, and the fissures of Cader looked deep and frosty. We paused for a moment near the bank, where the road takes its first deep drop. In the fields, half a mile below, the white-washed front of the longhouse glimmered palely in the half-light, but there was no welcome there—Kath and Iolo were away and the house was empty.

As we drove over the pass, the skyline stood out in a bold, black, sweeping silhouette, and we sped along in the gathering darkness in silence. As night came, one or other would fall asleep for an uneasy hour.

Towards midnight, as we swung round the many bends of our village street, there were no suggestions of lit rooms behind the blacked-out windows. It had been dark and quiet when we left ; it was dark and quiet when we returned. I had an odd feeling, as if the day just gone had no reality, and was perhaps an extra span, squeezed in imagination from the crack between midnight and the next day ; and the village still slept, waiting for morning.

CHAPTER II

BACK in Oxfordshire we discussed ways and means.

"For a time," said Mat, "we can live with tea-chests and packing-cases. After that—what?"

"After that," I said, "I'll make some furniture." She thought for a moment before asking,

"Why not now, then we shall have something ready for summer?"

"Where?" I enquired.

"In the spare bedroom."

"We'd better ask Ruth," I said. "She may not want the evening peace disturbed by chiselling and hammering."

But Ruth said, "I shan't mind—and anyhow it's so far from the sitting-room that I shan't hear it. What about shavings though?" she added tentatively. "Won't they get all over the house?"

"No," I promised, "nothing will come beyond the spare-room door."

"Or the window," added Mat. "We don't want our landlady to know. She looked like the sort of woman with definite ideas on what tenants may do. I don't think carpentry would be one of them!"

"Well then," said Ruth, "leave the curtains up so that it still looks like a bedroom—at any rate from outside."

It occurred to none of us that carpentry is a noisy industry, difficult to keep secret.

I visited the travelling county library, and found among its stock a book on elementary woodwork. In the spare room I sat and read it through twice from cover to cover—even the usual unnecessary preamble telling me, rather piously, of the sense of satisfaction I should get from making *something* with my own hands, be it only a nail box.

The chapter on choosing tools alarmed me. So many

things could be wrong. The maker of planes should, apparently, so arrange things that the grain of the wood used in them ran in a very definite direction. The steel of the blade must have been selected, treated and tempered in some way quite beyond the grasp of my understanding. The stock was to be properly seasoned. How was I to discern green from seasoned timber ? The whole chapter shouted : " Let the buyer beware ! " It seemed to me, after the second reading, that the simplest thing would be for Parliament to evolve some kind of legislation, laying down regulations for plane makers, as to what they should and should not use and do, when making their tools.

The following Saturday found me in Banbury. I examined the whole stock of planes carried by the first ironmonger I visited. Those planes could only have been made, according to my book, by an unscrupulous manufacturer, and bought by a retailer as incompetent and inexperienced in planes as myself. I took them, one after the other, to the doorway, and examined them critically in the daylight. The assistant seemed undecided as to whether I was a very high-class craftsman or a crackpot. At the next shop it was the same ; but I was assured that they were all from a very good maker, an aristocrat of the tool trade ; which made it, I thought, all the worse. *Noblesse Oblige.* At my third shop and last hope, the planes were all placed low in the window—craftily low I suspected by this time, in order to conceal their deficiencies. They were like the rest. Time was going. The village bus was due out in ten minutes, and on Saturdays it always had a very long queue. I hesitated for five of them, looking at the citizens of Banbury, and wondering what backing they would give to their M.P. if he brought in a private bill on laws relating to wooden plane making, and then I went in and bought a steel one. It felt, as it lay on my lap in the bus, solidly efficient ; at any rate it couldn't warp, and it solved my anxieties on grain.

In a London market-place—one of those fascinating Saturday morning markets that sell anything one can buy in a shop, and a good deal that one can't, I bought later, from a second-hand tool stall, a great steel plane two feet long.

It weighed ten and a half pounds, and I bought it because all the books I had read, proved conclusively that the longer the sole, the more accurate one's work would be. The books didn't tell me that using it for the first time would render me incapable of any further physical work for a week. The labour of pushing it was enormous. After using it for a month, I developed muscles of steel, for it needed a firm stance, lest, instead of my pushing it forward, it pushed me backward. I felt at the time that, if freakish circumstances arose requiring me to support a pyramid of acrobats on my prostrate form, I would have survived it.

Chisels too, gave me trouble. I played safe, as I thought, and selected a set with the aristocrat's name on their handles. When I got them home I found they all had blunt ends like screwdrivers. Indignantly I returned with them. Pityingly I was told that chisels were never sold sharpened. That was left to the user. "Why, I'm surprised he didn't know that," remarked the assistant.

I felt that some excuse was called for. "But he's only an apprentice yet," I said, apologetically.

"He ought to know that, all the same," he replied. "It's one of the first things they learn."

I bought my oilstone, and a fascinating oilcan that shot a spurt of oil for yards on pressing a lever. It had a wonderful length of throw, as I realized when I saw a long, spattered flick of oil staggering across the spare room ceiling.

Saws seemed comparatively easy to choose. For accurate work, and into this category I hoped mine would eventually fall, one used a tenon saw, and for rougher work, a handsaw with bigger teeth. The handsaw when I first began to use it, made alarming screeching noises, which I was afraid would carry as far as our landlady's house, and I hurriedly read up the law relating to tenancies. Furniture making by tenants was not mentioned as a reason for requiring a tenant to quit, so I tried the saw again. I stuffed rags in the cracks between the window sashes and persisted. I oiled it. It made no difference. I used it only when there was a pro-gramme of modern music by the B.B.C. downstairs, hoping it would be taken as part of the instrumentation by passers by. Occasionally as I pushed it back and forth, it made a sudden threatening noise like " WHOM ! " as it bent itself into a swift, tight bow, but it still remained whole. I suppose it had what is called " a good temper." After about a week of the excruciating screaming noises, I suddenly got the feel of it, and the protesting shrieks stopped. No one was more relieved than I, as I removed the rags, and let in much needed air.

Bu this time I had acquired a little more aplomb in my manner when choosing tools for the apprentice, and on to him I fobbed my likes and dislikes. The assistant would bring out his whole stock, and we became very chatty on whether the boy would rather have a straight or a skew back to his saws. On that visit, I got the only Disston saw they had had in for six months, for, as he said, " A young lad should start off with the right tools, and not get bad habits."

I agreed heartily, adding mentally that so should all ages and sexes, particularly someone starting late like myself, for I had less time in which to cure bad habits.

Panel pins and nails I bought by the pound, and screws by the gross, in little green-labelled cardboard boxes—not because I thought I should use screws by the gross, but because I liked the look of an acreage of the little boxes, with the contents arranged head to tail. I bought a " Record " combination plane, and spent a pleasant evening making all kinds of beadings and mouldings, before I gave up art for art's sake, and kept to the rebates and grooves for which it had been bought.

I collected a good selection of bits, including an expanding one which would bore a hole up to three inches in diameter. But the strength needed to bore holes three inches in diameter in hardwood was considerable, and on the evenings when I had such a job to do, we all assembled in the workshop, two hands pressing the brace down from above, and the other two of us trying to find enough room on the small sweep of it to put our four hands and turn.

It took a long time to find a gluepot more than toy size. They seemed to be as scarce as platinum frying-pans. It was Mat who was successful at last and again it was in a Saturday morning market-place. She returned late one Sunday evening, after a week-end at home. It was pouring with rain, and the cottage is a mile from the station. The door flew open and there was a loud metallic crash as she put the gluepot on the floor. She had left her suitcase at the station in order to carry it. It was about the size of a cauldron for a not quite full-sized witch. When I look at it now, I often wonder whether it really is a gluepot, or something that, in the intricacies of war, somehow got diverted from its rightful destination of cookhouse at Aldershot or Catterick. When one's eyes become accustomed to peering, one sees a small amount of glue, lying, like truth, deep at the bottom of a well, and after putting the pot on to heat, I know I can polish the floor or mow the lawn before it even begins to simmer. But it was made to last, and will probably be in use fifty years hence, unless by then, our furniture is of shining, soul-less plastic, having no joints and needing no glue.

I now began to consider how to make a bench with no bench to make it on, and omitting to buy the apprentice his usual tool, I went instead to a timber merchant. Here, a doddering old man with an absent manner and a rusty saw, made casual marks on the planks I had selected, and drawing a rough, unsquared line with his rule, began to saw crookedly across. I watched, alarmed. This went against all I had learnt. Sternly, I pointed out, that his line if he sawed to it, would lessen by a couple of inches, the length I wanted. He looked slowly up, gazed vaguely about him for a few seconds, and then said,

" Y' should 've allowed a few inches." I didn't see why I should pay for his wasted inches and said so, and we stood looking at each other for moments, neither of us saying anything. Then, leaving his saw still in the cut, he fetched from the office a large square, even rustier than the saw, and did the job properly. Whenever later, I visited him for any softwood I wanted, he would stare at me hazily for a few minutes before disappearing into the wooden shed to fetch out the square ready for the planks I tugged along. He bore no malice.

The kitchen copper, a permanent construction of brick,

offered the most solid base in the house on which to work. To help, I had Mat and a small cramp. Assisted to some small extent by the cramp, she held on to the wood as I planed it, occasionally jumping clear as the plane made a more determined sweep in her direction.

My early results were depressing. I set myself for a powerful sweeping stroke, anticipating a long, thin, delicately curving shaving falling to the floor. The reality was very different—a tremendous juddering and bucking of the plane along the surface, a lot of little chips like battered firewood on the floor, disastrously great holes rent in the grain of timber that had previously been, at any rate, approximately level, and a great exhaustion in me. The art of planing, like all other skills, came slowly.

For a long time the theory of dovetails was a mystery to me. I spent hours trying to see from drawings, how they were meant to fit, but " ever more came out by the same door as in I went." In dim, fleeting moments in which I helped out theory by dovetailing the fingers of both hands together, and often wringing them in despair, I began to see how it might be possible that two pieces of wood, each differently shaped, and with cuts at such odd angles, might yet be made to fit together. One night, it was divulged to me in a vision, and I suddenly saw how they worked.

Now that the theory was clear, I tried it out, and although I cannot say that it fitted in the cabinet-maker's sense of the word, I could see how, in time, I might make one that did. I filled in a slight gap with plastic wood. In course of time, I realized that plastic wood should have no place in a proper workshop, or at any rate, should not be used to fill gaps that should not be there, and with the realization, my joints began to fit without the need of plastic surgery. At the end of the week the bench was ready. I took it upstairs to the spare room, assembled it, and looked at it with pride. Had I dared, I would have suggested that we had tea on it. As it was, my first thought on waking for at least a week was, " I've made a bench—now I can go ahead and make the furniture."

Our spare cash was now diverted from tools to timber,

and I considered ways in which I could liquidate the apprentice. His kit, by now, was large enough for him to earn his
living unaided. He had, in any case become rather an
embarrassment of late, and my replies to the assistant's
queries as to his progress were becoming somewhat thread--
bare. I was afraid he might be asked to tea one Sunday,
so that the man could see for himself, and I hovered between
sending him as a journeyman to John o' Groats, or across
the Atlantic as a ship's carpenter. Actually I chose the
simpler and more ungrateful method of buying the few tools
I still needed in Oxford. Here the shopkeeper had a distant
manner, an " It's all the same to me " attitude, and tool
buying became easier. I could reject without having it
pointed out to me how unwise it was to jeopardize the boy's
career. All the same, it had been rather heart-warming, and
towards the end, I had felt that if I had expressed a feeling
that the boy was getting too expensive for me, I could almost
have been assured of his adoption by the Banbury ironmonger,
where he would have been given the run of the shop and
been thoroughly pampered.

We turned our minds to furniture. We would have liked
it to be of oak, for oak was in keeping with the tall woods
around Blaen-y-cwm, and with the gates and fences, beams
and stairs. But oak was too expensive for us ; we decided
on elm.

All the books were very discouraging about elm. It
warped badly and was never used in good class furniture.
As mine did not yet aspire to be first class, this worried me
less than the warping. That problem I solved by putting
the boards, as soon as we got them home, under our heaviest
furniture. It needed a very determined warp to lift a chest
of drawers. Another thing which swung our favour towards
elm, was that it could stand getting wet. The Rialto had a
foundation of a thousand or so elm-piles, and when they were
taken up they were found to be as sound as when they were
first driven in. London's first water pipes had been gouged
out of hollowed elm trunks. Thinking of my experiences of
boring three-inch holes, I reflected on what a dogged business
that must have been. The old Waterloo bridge had been

The Author

BLAEN Y CWM FROM THE BACK, WITH THE GARN ON LEFT, AND THE HOLLOW OF THE BARD'S CHAIR
ON CADER; GREEN LANE TO LEFT OF LOWER BARN

built on elm-piles, and finally, coffins were made from elm. What then, could be better for Wales, where our bottom fields were liable to flood, and the damp mists swathe the house?

Our cash now trickled into a supply of elm coffin-boards which I stored where I could. My friends were tolerant. At times, we breakfasted, dined and supped on a raised dais of coffin-boards. We clambered into high beds, up steps of coffin-boards. I was reminded of the man who nightly slept in his coffin, so as to give him a due sense of the ephemeral character of this world. As the month went on we sank to a less elevated position as the pile grew less. Just before timber went on licence, we almost made a corner in elm, all of us withdrawing what money we could spare, and sinking it in coffin-boards, and a singularly appropriate investment it seemed too, in those days of Dunkirk.

The timber yard was in a village a few miles away; a typical Cotswold village of lovely mellowed stone, in which every cottage, shop and building looked as though it had been there since time began and meant to stay there until time ceased. It was a peaceful place; I never went there without returning in a contented state of mind. We collected our boards, some with graceful, curling grain, some with little dark brown eyes in them like those in bird's-eye maple, and occasionally, Dutch elm with a lovely dark green streak in the pale brown. On the way back we'd call at the antique shop so that Mat could look at ear-rings, for to induce Mat to pass a shop selling ear-rings was, and is, as difficult a thing as to persuade a terrier to ignore a live rabbit. At the antique shop one day, we bought a beautiful copper plate. Fat, curving trout, embossed, chased each other round the rim. It hangs now in Blaen-y-cwm hall, polished each holiday to a deep, shining red-gold.

When we invested in elm in quantity, the storage problem became acute. To get some of the long planks indoors was a minor stevedoring work, for the front door of our cottage opened on to a narrow hall, rather like entering a T road, from a country lane. We couldn't turn the long boards for their destination of upstairs, as the open door blocked the turn. We had first to persuade them into the kitchen on the

B

right, and much paint was scraped off the door jambs doing this. We then shut the front door, and headed them back along the hall to the sitting-room at the other end. Here we could get sufficient turn on them to divert the front end upstairs. But some were too long or too broad even for this, and these we took round to the back of the house, and by a great deal of pushing from below, and pulling from above, and tense moments when they got out of reach of the pushers and wavered in the balance in the uncertain hands of the puller, we got them through the window to the landing, which was long and narrow like the hall. Here we stored them. They added an extra step up to our stairs, and an extra step down to our bedrooms. Until we grew used to them, there would be sudden heavy thuds in the dark, as someone, not remembering, stepped off on to a floor that was not there, or which was at any rate, inches below expectations.

How we expected to keep my occupation a secret I cannot imagine now ; we must have had much of the ostrich in our make-up ; but I repaired the front and back garden-gates, and made a rough shed for garden tools and bicycles, and as a result, our caution regarding the landlady relaxed. For such laudable efforts, which she could not help seeing, we felt our laurels should be sturdy enough for us to lean on them a little.

Planing these longer planks was a feat, for when they were laid on the bench, one end projected through the open door on to the landing, and the other end stopped just short of the window. I would take a step or two back, like a cricketer preparing to bowl, and then gallop through the open door, alongside the board, stopping just in time to prevent my twenty-four inch plane from crashing through the window. I had so many near misses, that eventually I took to planing with the window open. The novelty of seeing a pair of hands clutching a large plane shooting quickly through the window and back again drew many curious glances from passers-by, but as it became familiar, its interest palled and the village proceeded about its business without a look in our direction.

My promise that shavings would not leak beyond the spare

room door was as impossible a thing to achieve as to stop
snow from falling. Every evening as I finished work, I would
carefully remove all stray wisps from my apron, contorting
myself to reach all round. Then I combed any from my
hair, gave myself a final shake, opened the door a crack and
squeezed through. As soon as I got downstairs to the hall,
two or three shavings would be lying on the floor there. It
was an absolute puzzle. I became convinced that they
sneaked through between the window sashes as soon as I
had left, floated downstairs, opened the letter-box quickly,
got in and lay down. I made what amends I could by
making it my job to sweep landing, stairs and hall each day,
a dusty job I loathed.

Our old milkman, a one-time undertaker, was, for a long
time, silently but obviously mystified by the goings-on. One
morning he could bear it no longer. He waddled down the
path, a milk can hanging at each side of the wooden yoke he
carried, measured out our small quota into the jug, and then
burst out with :

" I see coffin-boards a-goin' in, goin' in. What be you
a-doin' with them all ? I never see coffin comin' out."
Fortunately, he never did.

I made most of the furniture on the pegged pattern for
two reasons. First, it could be packed flat, and sent off to
be assembled at Blaen-y-cwm with its pegs. The Taoist
philosophy expresses my feeling about it very well :

" The clay is moulded to make a pot
And the pot fits round nothing.
Herein lies the usefulness of the pot.
Doors and windows are pierced in the walls of a house
And they fit round nothing ;
Herein lies the usefulness of a house.

Thus it is, while it must be taken as advantageous
To have something there,
It must also be taken as useful to have nothing there."

and in the case of the furniture packages, it was desirable
to squeeze out even the nothing, until the time came to put
it back again. The second reason for pegging wherever

I could, instead of merely glueing, was my fear that the long periods when it stood in a damp and empty house, would soften the glue in the joints and loosen them, so that they would drop to pieces, and we should arrive to find large heaps of warped coffin-boards on the stone floor.

As Whitsuntide approached, we had accumulated a few things to go to Blaen-y-cwm. Mat was to take them in her Morris, a car in which, as she pointedly said, she need not sit on the floor to drive, taking with her, her sister, a couple of shelter mattresses, and as much stuff as we had amassed, or alternatively, as much as would go in. So much went in that her passenger had to get out up the hills and walk to the top.

I was to spend Whitsuntide bird-watching with Kath in her home-county of Herefordshire, an arrangement made long before we had heard of Blaen-y-cwm. It was by no means the scientific kind of expedition, in which one tabulates all in a little notebook at the end of each day, but just a casual ambling around fields and orchards with binoculars, poking about in shady streams for moorhen and mallard, occasionally varied by paddling, and turning over stones quickly to catch bullheads, and sometimes just lazing away a hot afternoon by lying on the bank watching kingfishers whistle by and walking home with the scent of beanfields heavy in the evening air.

I had two almost illegible letters from Mat. Much muscular effort on beam-scraping must have preceded them, for her usually firm writing wandered about weakly, like the long, thin legs of the spiders that we sometimes find marooned in our bath.

The idea behind the Whitsuntide visit was that Mat should scrape the whitewashed beams, ceiling, walls, and everything scrapeable, so that we could go straight ahead in summer, stain the beams, and distemper everything—everything, that is, that one usually distempers. So much, and of such thickness seemed to be coming off that I wondered whether our floor measurements would still be even approximately correct. I think she added several cubic feet to the interior air space.

A disheartening and weary task that scraping must have been—perched on the rungs of a heavy farm ladder, so worn that they cut into the feet, arms constantly stretched up and aching, eyes peering into the cobwebbed corners, dust and flaking limewash falling upon the upturned face, teeth forever gritting on the floating particles of lime and cement in the dusty air. Then, after she had descended and laboriously shifted the ladder to set it up further along, an unscraped portion would disclose itself on the piece just finished, and down she would get to heave the ladder back again.

The weather was glorious in both Wales and Herefordshire —a week of blazing sun, but except for a couple of hours of social discourse, and tea with Iolo, who staggered up on a broiling hot afternoon with a pair of steps on his shoulders, the whole of Mat's week went in scraping.

They lived by the frying-pan, and Enid's immense loaves, and when darkness came, and it was impossible to see any longer into the corners between the beams, they crawled up to the damp dormitory of a bedroom to their floor mattresses. A few scrawled lines as a P.S. told me that the situation was even lovelier than we had thought, and that the house really would begin to come up to our expectations and hopes by the end of the summer.

I gathered, however, that progress in the summer would be much quicker if we had a little more comfort in the way of furniture, so on my return from Herefordshire I started on a cupboard and a table. The cupboard was a poor thing because I knew no better. Its joints were wrong. In summer it works well enough, but after a damp winter when the doors swell and the rusty lock refuses to turn, the only way to get into it is to hit off the top with a mallet. Still— better to have a top that hits off when desired, than sides that fall down whether desired or not, as would have been the case with my loose joints had not the top held them together. The framework was filled in with plywood, and I sometimes look at it now and ponder on changing ideas of economy, for at that time it could be bought in large sheets for small sums.

About this time, I came across George Sturt's " Wheel-wright's Shop," and Walter Rose's " Village Carpenter "—two books which delighted me. I was considerably cheered, too, to read somewhere else that elm, properly seasoned and stored, unstained, but rubbed with linseed oil and polished with beeswax, made very attractive furniture. There were pictures too, of shining old settles, tables and panelling.

Seeing these pictures, and reading these books by craftsmen, I now saw myself as a sort of village Chippendale, turning out fine elm pieces, sought out and fought for by dis-criminating collectors. So far, I have not been troubled by collectors—but was Chippendale ?

The size and shape of the table caused us considerable thought, but the question settled itself when we went into Oxford for our weekly bath. Our cottage bath—as a bath —was a menace. A forgetful user had only absent-mindedly to lift the plug, forgetting that we had no plumbing system, to flood the house, and it had seemed safer to buy a tin bath. Quite soon we gave that up too. Both had to be filled and emptied by hand. The attendant at the Oxford baths, when we explained our plight, used to let us in on Saturday morning—men's day. Even so, we seemed to be the only early morning users. Perhaps all the men in Oxford have baths of their own. Before going home, we went to a small restaurant for coffee, and as we sat drinking it, it struck me that our table was rather nicely proportioned. I looked at it carefully and tried to memorize it. We all had a guess at its measurements, and we all differed wildly. A week later, we returned. In my pocket was my steel measuring-tape. Unfortunately, at one end of the table—it would seat six—was an elderly, severe-looking man, reading *The Times*, which lay on the cloth in front of him. I couldn't do my measuring without disturbing him, and I didn't want to ask him to lift his paper so that I could, as this would involve explanation and he looked the " never-apologize-never-explain " sort. As we sat down, he lifted his *Times*, and quite blotted himself out. I expect he felt annoyed, that in an almost empty café three women should choose his table. We must have appeared to him like the

motorists who come and park behind one on a long rolling
stretch of unparked-on moorland road.

We ordered coffee, and I brought out the tape. As I carefully unwound it, it made a disconcerting " click, click," like
the free wheel of a bicycle. I had never noticed this trait
before. I quickly measured the leg length, and the width
of the top, but to get the length was not so easy. It seemed
a terribly long table. I stealthily edged out more and more
steel inches, with more and more clicks, and had almost
reached *The Times*, when the waitress brought our coffee.
I suddenly felt guilty. At that moment, measuring a table
seemed to rank in iniquity with making notes and measurements of fortifications. I pressed the spring, and the tape
shot back with a great clatter and final resounding click.
The sharp metallic noise at each revolution sounded like
machine-gun fire in that quiet place.

The waitress jumped, and looked at us suspiciously, but we
were all looking, over-casually, in other directions. I let a
minute or two elapse, and then, recovering my nerve, paid
out the tape once more. It had nearly reached the far end,
and Mat, anxious to help the business on, gently stretched
out her hand and pushed it, giving *The Times* a slight shiver
as she did so. Its owner peered over the top of it, and we
all looked back at him like apprehensive children. His gaze
went slowly down to the table where the long, shining steel tape
stretched along to him. His eyes travelled down the length
of it to me holding the other end. I felt I was holding a
time-fuse which was already touched off. He looked at me
coldly and enquiringly, and this so unnerved me that I
accidentally pressed on the button, and the thing leapt away
from him like a swift steel serpent, and coiled itself savagely
into my hand. He folded his paper and just sat, staring in
front of him.

" I'm so sorry," said Ruth conversationally. " We were
just measuring the table." But he made no reply, and
just went on looking coldly into space, while we talked
to each other on whatever subjects we could manage to
muster.

The waitress brought his bill at last, and he got up and

left. The place was fairly full now ; and I still hadn't got the length. The waitress eyed us each time she passed.

" Ask her," whispered Mat, as she gave us our bill. So I asked, and very silly it sounded.

" Do you mind if I measure the table ? " In the quietness, the question seemed to echo round the room. The waitress looked uncertain as to whether she had heard aright, but having made the first step, I meant to get those measurements before I left. I repeated the question. She made a noise in her throat which I chose to take as permission, and disappeared quickly—to tell the manageress, I expect. But before she had reached the door, the job was done, and we were on our way out, watched by all the visible pairs of eyes and several odd single ones through the crack of the service door.

With my hopes buoyed up by the pictures in the books, I finished the table with linseed oil and beeswax. Linseed oil has a tenacious smell, and at oiling times it became for me what the perfume manufacturers call, " Your own distinctive perfume ". Mat, on one of her visits home, had brought back from the Charing Cross Road a tattered little volume on stains, paints and polishes, published in the nineteenth century. It spoke of exotic ingredients such as Alkanet root, Red Sanders, Fustic, Turmeric, Persian Berries, Nut Galls, Catechu, Thus, Sandaric, Amber and Dragon's Blood. In it, I read that a brick wrapped in flannel makes the best possible polisher for linseed oil. We kept our eyes open for bricks lying about in the village, but it was a stone village, and no one seemed to have had any need of bricks, or if they had, had felt that they were rare and precious articles, not to be left carelessly lying about.

As a substitute, we selected the nicest heavy stone with one flat surface that we could find on the allotments wall, removed it at dusk, and wheeled it home in the barrow under cover of fork, spade and rake. This we not only wrapped in flannel ; we swaddled it in flannel, and finally sewed it up in a pair of old flannel pyjamas.

Every morning, noon and evening the table had its rub. The heavy polisher lay on it ready for any spare moment's work. Whoever finished her housework first gave it its morning rub. Whoever had the bicycle and reached home first in the dinner-hour gave it another vigorous ten minutes, but in the evenings it was a purely voluntary occupation. I seem to remember that we suggested that it would be a suitable work for Ruth in her convalescence from quinsies, and when friends stayed with us, we managed, by various roundabout methods, to get them to rub it too, implying that rubbing a table was a unique experience, not to be missed if one were ever lucky enough to get the chance of it. I dare say if I had taken it to school and worked on the matter in the manner of Tom Sawyer whitewashing fences, I could have washed my hands of it entirely.

Before the summer term was ended we sent it off by train, along with the cupboard, and as much of the dairy furniture as I had managed to finish. We hoped to find it waiting for us when we arrived in Wales.

CHAPTER III

THE summer holidays came, and I started off for my first holiday at Blaen-y-cwm. Mat had a wedding in the family and would not be able to join me for several days. The Singer was full of saucepans and hardware, and the whole trip was a clatter of tinny noises and occasional bell-like clangs as a saucepan found a more comfortable position, and on high ground there was an eerie whistling of wind through the planks towering in the boot.

The first night I stayed at the longhouse, for Kath was going to leave her comfortable haven there to come and stay with me and a few of my earlier pieces. I was grateful for this, for I was not sufficiently familiar with Blaen-y-cwm to feel quite at ease at the thought of spending a holiday alone in a house that had itself been alone for so long, and from whose windows no other habitations were visible. One must know a house and its surroundings and, above all, its noises, before one can be happy in it alone. And the noises of Blaen-y-cwm in its early days were startling, not to say alarming.

In the quietness of the evening the oven door, without warnings or preliminaries, would burst sharply open on its one unbroken hinge. Or a gale would suddenly rise from nowhere, tearing up through the little wood with a deep and swelling roar, and then—taking three quiet seconds to cross the open space to the barn—it would seize the loose, rusting sheets of corrugated roofing on the lean-to shed, and shake them with demoniacal fury. It moaned and shrieked and whistled through the holly tree in a manner no B.B.C. effects-man has ever achieved. When it blew from the mountains behind, it would seethe through the dry stone-walling at the back, flinging open the door, to send it crashing against the wall. In the night, as one lay awake listening to it tearing over the roof and wondering how firmly the chimneys were cemented on, there would be the slither and fall of a tile sliding from the barn roof to the stones below, or a sharp series of cracking noises from the landing floor, followed by a most deep and blood-curdling groan as the bedroom door was pressed open upon its rusty strap-hinges. Then there were alarming animal noises. The first sheep with a cough that I ever heard lay beneath the bedroom window on a still night, and the sudden racking, unfamiliar sound made my hair stand on end! It was a noise such as a ghost, agonizingly coming to life, might have made. The stream, too, sometimes sounded like people muttering beneath the window.

I was glad then when Kath suggested spending a few days with me, for Kath loves the mountains, never minds how much it rains, is very accommodating about what she eats, takes pleasure in washing at a stream where there is no bathroom, and is perfectly happy so long as there is enough to read. She suffers in fact from what Iolo calls " printitis ", for she will painstakingly peel a tattered, yellow, twelve-months'-old newspaper wrapping from packed furniture legs in order to read last year's news. She was also one of the few people I could ask to stay in a house which was in the unusual position of having most of its furniture lying about loose, as legs, pegs, stretchers and tops.

Next morning we walked up to Blaen-y-cwm, laden with my more portable packages. Rain had fallen the whole night through, and it was doubtful whether the car would go up the fields for new streams were rushing down the mountainside, and the old ones had risen and were taking shorter cuts down slopes unused in dry weather. Before we had been out for fifteen minutes we were soaked. But it was warm rain, and we walked happily enough up the hill. Summer was full blown, and loosestrife was blooming beyond the pink farm. Kath stopped and looked at it with the rain dripping off nose, eyebrows and chin.

" They'd look lovely by your stream," she said. " Let's dig a few roots and carry them up." I undid a parcel, its wrappings already soggy and disintegrating, and took out a screwdriver. Dropping on sodden knees into the sodden bog, we excavated little canals around the roots, and pulled up half a dozen plants. I was wearing my new tough, hand-made Robert Laurie shoes, and this last soaking added to the trickle of water which ran into them from the bottom of my mac., caused them to squelch unpleasantly. For shoes to become wet from the outside in is one matter, but to become wet from the inside out, seemed unnatural, and too much to expect even the best of shoes to weather. As I walked little bubbles were squeezed out through the welt, and it struck me as too harsh a treatment for them. I took them and my wet socks off, and walked barefooted on the soft grass.

As we dug the plants in by the side of the stream I visual-ized them in a few years' time—score upon score of tall red spires. But it was only the first of so many disappointments. The sheep ate them, as the sheep have eaten everything else that we have tried to grow. Red spires may be growing in the fields they have just left, and they have turned up their small, sheep noses at them ; but as soon as they are planted in the green enclosures by the house they become, to their small sheep minds, infinitely delectable.

When we had put in the plants, we unlocked the house door and entered, stepping straight into a pool of water which had blown under the great gap at the bottom of it. I lit a fire in the damp grate, and put on some of the wood that Mat had collected at Whitsuntide. Then we took off our clothes, wrung them out, and changed into drier, if not dry clothes.

We fetched water from the waterfall at the stone trough and put the kettle on to boil, and by it, at the side, we cooked chops and chips in the same pan. We ate them sitting on upturned boxes by the fire, and as I neared the end of mine, it struck me that Kath seemed to be receding into the dis-tance. I looked at the rest of the room. The dresser was scarcely visible, and the window a dim grey patch seen through a thick pall of fog. My heart sank. The chimney smoked ! By opening the door and creating a draught, helped on by waving sheets of plywood in the air, we dis-persed most of it and shut the door. Smoke immediately began to eddy about the ceiling again. We opened the door and it disappeared. We shut it and it began again. It smoked horribly. In a few minutes, thick wood smoke, so fragrant outside in small quantities, so acrid inside in large, had filled the room and reduced the already small amount of light reaching us from the misty world outside. There was nothing for it but to leave the door open, and endure the cold draught that poured down from the mountain. We strung our wet clothes across the open doorway, hoping that at any rate the draught would benefit them, but there are, I discovered that day, dry draughts and damp draughts, and we found then, as we have found so often since, that nothing hung up to dry on a day when mists are in the valley dries at all unless it is directly over a blazing fire.

Kath settled down on her box to read, and I went up to the dim bedroom to make it a little more habitable. Dark came early, and we had tea on that summer afternoon, at about five o'clock, in a rapidly deepening murk. Wrapped in eiderdowns, we sat reading by the light of a single-wick oil-lamp. I read Dorothy Pilley's account of a Christmas spent in the Snowdon hut, and as I read, our plight seemed similar, if not so intense. I tried hard to remember what Blaen-y-cwm had looked like in May, and to recall the passages in Mat's letters describing the appearance of the place in the sunny week at Whitsuntide. In the quietness, two tiny field mice came out from the cavernous recess beneath the bread-oven, and ran along the hearth eating our crumbs, little disturbed when we raised our heads or moved our feet.

We went to bed early, hoping to be warmer and more comfortable there, but either the two mice accompanied us, or the rest of the family lived upstairs, for all night long there were tiny squeakings and scamperings and rustlings as they probed into the paper wrappings of packages lying on the floor. We slept on mattresses on the floor and Kath said she didn't mind the mice so long as they didn't actually run over her. As it was difficult to convey this information to them, I kept them on the run for short spaces, by firing up the chimney an air pistol which I had brought with me in the car on the night journey. I always hoped it would give me moral, if no other kind of courage, in case of trouble. Towards dawn, I stopped worrying about the mice. We didn't have much sleep that night, neither did the mice. Consequently, when morning came, we were all very weary, and Kath and I at any rate, slept on until about eleven o'clock.

Kath woke first, and peering through the small, many-paned window, informed me that it was a wonderful morning, with Cader in full view, wisps of diaphanous cloud floating across the sky, and hot sun drying the cwm. It was. The sheep and their lambs lay contentedly in the little fields, the black bullocks scratched their necks on the gate posts. The streams, which yesterday had foamed in cataracts, were now mere streaks falling lazily to the valley below. The rocks were dry and clean and grey in the sun. There was no wind. It was a perfect summer morning.

We got up, hung a line between the gnarled plum trees, and put our clothes out to dry. We opened all the windows to let the warm air pour through the house, after which we sat outside the front door and ate a leisurely breakfast, approached by inquisitive lambs, who came with hesitant, delicate steps almost to the door, warned only at the last moment by some sixth sense, to retreat from these two creatures that neither mother nor experience had taught them to deal with.

We explored the big wood, finding it a beautifully mossy, bouldered place. To the south lay the long ridge of Cader ; opposite us were the rocky sides of Y Garn and behind, the crags of Mynydd Mynach swept to the north. As the crests towered towards the lake, they grew higher and became more majestic ; the skyline changed and soared to Diphwys, to Llethr, and finally to the dramatic gap of the Rhinogs.

In the wood, the sunlight pierced the straggly tops of the overgrown oaks, and shone, bright and dappled, on the grey boulders and cushions of moss. Ferns hung from the limbs and trunks of the aged trees. Intense black depths of shadow lay in oddly shaped pools beneath the overhang of the rocks, and on their southern facing sides, grey lichens crept, in strange map-like patterns.

We wandered up the small easterly cwm towards the mass of rock that juts steeply up and away from the main ridge, and is called " Craig-y-Deryn "—Rock of the Birds. Ring-ousels had nested there on a heather-grown crag ; for most of the day, the vigilant male, perched above, kept watch, starting his piercing alarm note while we were yet a quarter of a mile away. We crossed the moor back to the main stream and waded its turbulent course beneath dark, over-hanging branches, clutching our long ash poles to probe the bed and discover the drops into deeper pools before we found them by the more startling method of falling into them. We strolled to the small top wood, looking for nests and finding some—of both wood-pigeon and magpie, and higher up the stream, climbing over the loose and awkward wall dividing us from the mountain proper, came to a wild little ravine, its upper end closed by a view of Diphwys. High up there, in the solitary wind-blow hawthorn was the nest of a carrion crow. The curlew called from the further bog all day long, a lovely, long, melancholy, bubbling sound like woodwind, and the croak of the ravens came from far away, an unmistakable " Glog, Glog," carrying faintly on the wind from the slopes of Llethr.

Blaen-y-cwm, as we washed in the stream, was very different from Blaen-y-cwm of the previous night. The flat stones in front of the door were warm to my bare feet long after the sun had dropped behind the mountain, as I stood watching the light on Cader change from deep gold to pale gold, and from pale gold to grey. We walked down to fetch milk in the dusk, treading softly to avoid disturbing the dogs, and thankful to find them all away rounding up sheep. As we came back, the sky was the clear, deep blue that sometimes comes after sunset on a June or July evening, a colour which, seen from a lamp-lit room looks so vivid and yet so transparent in its brightness, that it seems the sun is somewhere behind it still.

For the last hour before going to bed, we lit a fire. It blazed up quickly, and the shadows of the packing cases leapt up and down on the wall. I shut the door. It seemed to me, after such a day as we had had, no fire would have the temerity to smoke—nor did it. Even the mice were quiet that night.

We woke early. Mat was arriving on the afternoon train, and we started early to meet her, as, on the way, I wanted to see Willie. " Willie," I said, " I'm going to buy a bag of cement, but I don't want to take it up the bog track in the car as we are so heavily loaded. If I fetch it up the valley and leave it here, can you bring it up sometime ? "

" Cement," he said, " why, yes, of course. I'll bring it up to-night with Twm and the cart when I've done the milking. Any job like that, or any parcels to fetch from the station, that I shall be glad to do." During our settling-in —a prolonged business—Willie and his cart were invaluable.

Cement was always one of our most precious commodities. It could do so much. Because of this, it has always had the greatest consideration when packing up time has come. It was always given the best place to sit, the warmest and dryest wrappings folded around it, and the best bedroom to stay in until we came again. It has always had these things since the time we arrived and found the hundredweight sack so laboriously brought up and carried in, turned into a solid fossil-like object, strangely patterned by the creases in the paper bag, and utterly useless.

We continued down the valley to have lunch with Iolo, and two hours before Mat's train was due, I went into Dol-gelley alone for the bag of cement.

From the estuary, as I drove back, the mountains looked very lovely. The water was calm and mirror-like and from the toll-bridge road, the reflections of the whitewashed inn beside the water lay clear and unruffled in Penmaenpool below, The little house of the toll-bridge keeper stood perched on its stilts in the muddy sand. Swans floated with the current below the bridge, and further down were a few oyster catchers, their red legs looking even redder in the sunshine. The toy station seemed asleep, and one would have thought that no more trains were expected that day. I drove over the level crossing and parked the car by the goods shed, wondering whether the furniture had arrived, and peering through the crack in the door, tried to recognize my hessian parcel.

There was a sudden break in the quiet, a distant clanking

THE WAY TO OUR BRIDGE; THE CANOL LANE

BLAEN Y CWM FROM THE LAST FIELD; CRAIG Y DERYN, LITTLE CWM AND OAK WOOD ON EXTREME RIGHT

along the line, and creaking noises of wire controls as the train was signalled. Our from the ticket office came the station master in gold-braided cap.

" A van-full for you in the waiting-room," he called as he walked up the platform to take the tally from the driver.

" I'll ask Willie to collect it next time he comes down," I said. Out stepped the only passenger, and we and the cement proceeded up the valley. We collected our milk and post ; we had already said at the post office that we should not expect our post delivered beyond Cwm Mynach Isaf— Willie's farm, for it would have added almost an hour to the postman's already strenuous day.

A can of milk is a difficult thing to carry in a car along a track on which one can only lurch, and it is a harder job still when the carrier has to open all the gates. To enter the Singer at any time requires agility. The best way is to put in one leg, duck one's head and quickly collapse. One should then be on the seat. But one cannot do that carrying a can of milk, so that at every gate the milk was handed to me while Mat got out and opened it, handed back to her while I drove through, handed back to me while she got in, and handed back to her until the next gate. The final five minutes demands great skill from the milk carrier, for the track ascends and descends two small switchbacks in quick succession, and they both lie at different angles. Consequently, for two seconds, it feels as though giant hands have taken and wrung the car, and when they have finished, the bonnet is pointing upwards, obscuring the driver's view. This is inconvenient, for there is a line of boulders to be dodged before the spurt to surmount two large humps between the posts supporting the shed. Having gained sufficient momentum to do this, one is then inside and brakes quickly to avoid going through the wall. I defy anyone to carry milk and spill none under such conditions.   The nearest solution is to carry a quart of milk in a gallon can.

After tea, we took the things from the car and swung them up over the stone wall and wire-netting fence to the other side. When all was safely in, we went round the house inspecting each room minutely, and deciding what repairs and decorations each would need. My first day there had made me very conscious of draughts, and a windy, wheezy voice seemed to be shouting at me from every room— " Cement up that hole. Put a sill under the door. Mend that gaping hole in the window-frame."

In the small bedroom we had a satisfactory stack of paint and distemper brushes, trowels, plaster of Paris, distemper and paint. I longed to hear the " slap slap " of a distemper brush on those walls, and to smell new paint on the woodwork.

Twenty years empty had had its effect. As we wandered from room to room, we felt that twenty-one might have been just a year too long. The many new patches on the roof where Willie had repaired it, said only too plainly, " Here was a leak," leading us to fear that the beams and joists were rotted too. In the big bedroom, a large pattern of irregular brown scallops ran along the edge where rain had penetrated the plaster. A hole in the ceiling of the second bedroom had been patched with a piece of plywood from a tea-chest, its black-stencilled lettering clearly visible under a thin coat of whitewash. In one corner, the wall was covered with scribbled arithmetical calculations, bearing testimony to the size of the wool clip of years long gone, the pencilled pounds and shillings beside it denoting its owners hopes and fears. It must have been the last tenant's account book, and poring over it, one could have read the history of his good years and his bad. Most of the doors were wormeaten, and in the floor were two sets of holes, roughly circular and about an inch wide, through which one could peer into the hall and discover what was going on there without the bother of going down. They intrigued me for a long time.

" Ah," said Willie, when I asked him, " they were for ropes—put through to tighten the bales of wool on the ceiling below."

In the kitchen, the panels had disappeared from the built-in cupboard doors, and someone had attempted to cover paint of a dreary green with shiny cream paint which had run in streaks and left the dreary green still showing underneath.

The back of the house was in the worse condition. I have already commented on the amount of air that poured into it. There was no ceiling, only the sloping, plastered roof-beams. Chunks of plaster had dropped, and the breezes rushed straight in under the slates or through the numerous routes in the walls.

The guttering beneath the edge of the front roof occurred only spasmodically. Great spaces between each section allowed the water to cascade off each end and pour down the front of the house. The drainpipe which should have carried the water from the gutter which should have been there, reached about five feet down and then ended, leaving whatever water flowed down it to its own devices for the rest of the way. And in windy weather, with what glee it emerged from that little pipe! Exhilarated by its freedom after those narrow confines, it blew upwards in joyous fountains, and sprayed happily through the bedroom window.

Outside, at the foot of the holly tree, and along all the little walls, hordes of nettles had sprung up thickly since May, and in the nettles were collections of old scythe blades, rusty saws and broken farm implements, pieces of crockery, jam and pickle jars, sheep dip tins, containers for marking fluid, old marking irons corroded out of shape, tongs, pokers, broken ends of metal bedsteads, a fifty-six pound weight from a pair of scales with the beam and one pan, tangled rusty wire, bottomless buckets and piles of old ashes.

Thus described, it sounds like a slum. But it was not—merely an old farmhouse from which no one had troubled for a quarter of a century to clear away the accumulated rubbish. It was to us still the lovely house in a lovely cwm that had delighted us when we first saw it and given us pleasure whenever we had thought of it since. I could visualize those walls under clean primrose distemper with shining elm furniture ranged round them, the floors dry and clean and carpeted, the woodworm paraffined and dead, the woodwork painted, the nettles uprooted and the rubbish cleared away.

Slowly, except for the woodworm, these things became facts, but the process of repair and rejuvenation has no end.

Every holiday a new patch of roof is made weather-proof ; something else is done to floor, doors and windows. There lies one of the pleasures—it is never finished, and between the end of one holiday and the beginning of the next, one can think of all kinds of glorious new ideas on alterations and repairs. There is a pleasure, too, in feeling that one old house is being saved from becoming another deserted ruin in the valley.

Twm and the cart clattered into the yard before we went to bed, and Willie made short work of the stones propping the gate ; with the knack that seems inherent in those who have much to do with stone, he seemed to roll them aside with easy skill rather than great strength. As he dumped the cement-bag in the hall, I asked him where he had got his sand for repairs. He waved his hand airily towards the mountain.

" Up there," said he, " beneath the turf you will find plenty of good sand. I dug there in April when we mended your roof."

Next morning we were out prospecting for sand early. With pick, shovel, and a couple of buckets, we started up the slope behind the house. The course of the little stream providing our water supply had cut a deep channel for itself, or perhaps the channel had been cut for it, to bring the stream past the house. Whichever it was, there was the channel, and we thought we might, by walking alongside it, see the various layers through which it ran, and recognize the sand strata. But the whole bank was of dark solid peat about three feet deep. It looked a forbiddingly dense kind of soil to dig through, and I rather hoped the sand was not beneath it.

" Let's dig back the sides," suggested Mat. " We can't see what is behind it until we do." I drove the spade in, and with difficulty drew up a spadeful of the thick, black earth. While I dug deeper, Mat worked around the hole with the pick, and when we had emptied a sizeable hole and were still bringing up peat, we felt it was time to give up and try a more rewarding spot. We moved away to the smaller top wood where the grass had a different texture. There we dug again and brought up hundreds of small stones. It looked more hopeful ; small stones might easily turn into sand lower down. It seemed a logical sort of development. Deeper and deeper our hole went, producing more and more small stones, then bigger ones, and then very big ones indeed. At this rate we were in reverse and the sand ought to have been on top. It wasn't. We turned over the sods of the top spit very carefully, and found that their nourishment came from small stones only. We left the slopes and tried the level areas. They were no use. We dug in the wood, we scooped pebbles from the streams, hoping that perhaps the sand had settled beneath them. We tried the yard, we crossed the main stream and went nearly to the top track, dragging buckets and spade and pick and thinking what a simple job it must be to do a little cementing in the Sahara. But perhaps the Sahara has no cement.

After three hours of this, we saw that we must attack the problem more scientifically. Leaning by the stable loft steps was a heavy crowbar, and under the shed I had noticed a beetle—a tool like a heavy long-handled mallet, used for knocking in stakes. We started out again with these two implements, a chair from the Gladstone-Disraeli room, and a thimble firmly tied to a long stiff piece of wire.

We were going to make borings. Immediately behind the house we drove our first bore. Standing on the chair, and with Mat rather hesitantly holding the crowbar, I swung the beetle high into the aid and brought it down on to the end of the crowbar, one mighty blow following another, driving it in as far as it would go. It had seemed a good idea in theory ; in practice it was harder than digging. It was hard work to get the crowbar in ; it was very hard work to get it out again. Now for the sample. I lowered the thimble as far as it would go, and scraped it up the sides. It was disappointing, for the sides were very hard where blows with the crowbar had compressed the earth. After several more fruitless explorations with the thimble, Mat at last brought up half a dozen irritated looking ants. We emptied them carefully down the hole again, hoping they would alight at the right stop. Looking for a needle in a

haystack must be a simple task as compared with looking for
sand in that valley. After all—there is the haystack and
there is the needle. If one keeps patiently on, the needle
must turn up sometime, for a haystack is so much smaller
than a valley.

We gave up the hope of sand and went in to a meal, convinced that the nearest sand was at the seashore six miles
away, and while we washed up, decided that the only thing
to do was to go to Barmouth and get it. The sack of cement
sat at the end of the hall—a shapeless white elephant.
Obviously, we must get sand somehow. Careful calculations
before the holiday had shown us that we should have enough
petrol to get to Wales and back, and perhaps manage two
of our weekly shopping expeditions. In the stern face of
necessity, we must do all our shopping on foot, and the
petrol must take us to Barmouth for sand.

We reached the seaside in the height of the season, at
about four o'clock. Judging from the number of people
there, every boarding-house landlady must have said :

" This will be a lovely afternoon for a picnic. If I pack
tea for you, you will be able to stay down on the sands
until evening."

We took a short trip along the promenade, and were
depressed by the number of people covering up the sand ;
not quite so thickly as at Blackpool perhaps, but much too
thickly for our object, which we wished to attain as unobtrusively as possible. I thought of " Through the Looking-
Glass " :

> " The Walrus and the Carpenter
>   Were walking hand in hand :
>   They wept like anything to see
>   Such quantities of sand :
>   ' If only this were cleared away '
>   They said, ' It would be grand ! ' "

We drove slowly back, intending to try the harbour road,
thinking it would be quieter there ; but before we had gone
very far, we saw on the road and pavement, quite a large

amount of sand washed up by the high tides. A notice on a wooden board stated that to collect a load of sand from the foreshore would cost a pound. But a load was more than we needed, and certainly more than we could carry, for all we had brought were six small sandbags. Two little boys were building an enormous sand castle on the beach below. I wondered whether we could inveigle them into building it on the back seat, decided against it, and turned to considering the notice again. I felt it was rather thoughtless of Barmouth not to have added, " But those helping to keep the town tidy, by clearing up sand which is washed on to the promenade *from* the foreshore, are welcome to small quantities free." We discussed it, and decided that it was probably what they meant, and although their intention was not yet made public, I felt they would not mind us anticipating their generosity.

I placed the car between a block of tall, inquisitive-looking boarding-house windows, and the sand. We sat on the running board looking vaguely out to sea, idly playing with the sand as we watched the visitors go by. As soon as they had passed, we were industriously scooping up sand into our little bags. It seemed very odd not to have to dig for it. As a new group came in sight, we fell back into dreamy inactivity, and as the last pair of heels went across, we scrabbled furiously again, until our sandbags lay bulging on the back seat.

We drove home, swelled with a sense of achievement. I like Barmouth, especially in the winter, when it has more sand than people. I hope it bears us no grudge for removing the sand washed from its foreshore. They had such quantities, as the Walrus said. And we only took a little.

CHAPTER IV

THE flavour of breakfast bacon and egg still lingered as we surveyed the floors next morning, looking for the largest flat slab on which to mix cement. We chose one underneath Gladstone, as he looked approvingly down, remembering, I daresay, his own leisure occupations at Hawarden. Three buckets of sand and one of cement made an appreciable-sized heap, and mixing it we found heavy work. Dry, it was not so bad, but as more and more water was added, the shovelfuls got heavier and heavier, and irritating little rivulets of water kept escaping and had to be dammed off by a quickly slung shovelful of dryer material, and the removal of this would open up the escape route for another river. What an amount of water cement will take ! What thirsty stuff it is ! I grew tired of tipping up the ewer. And yet, how definitely it knows when it has had enough.

" Oh, the little more and how much it is." Far, far too much : a stiff intractable mass is turned immediately into a running disaster,—to be mopped up quickly with more cement and sand.

I started by trying to fill in great holes around the kitchen window. For the first half-hour there was no variation in the procedure. I put the cement on, and then quickly held the board underneath to field it as it fell off.

At the top of the window was a hole in a sort of overhang —and here I almost met my Waterloo. I tried all kinds of wiles, but after a second of suspense, out it dropped, caught just in time on the board. I became very good at that part of the business—so good that it was monotonous. I tried working faster, and the plops became faster too. I stooped to putting it in with my fingers, and the spatterings fell on my upturned face. Then I attempted a whole handful, and stroked it persuasively. It behaved as before. It was like wrestling with gravity. Then I began to get angry and

thought that if I could be quick enough and fling the whole
lot up at once, I might be able to stand and hold the board
underneath until it set. I hacked a large slice from the
pile and threw it savagely at the hole. To my great surprise,
it went in ; to my greater surprise, it stayed. It behaved
like some people, to whom one has to be nasty before they
will be nice. I threw in another lot, and another and
smoothed it well down with the trowel. It worked. I had
the knack. My only complaint was that the board became
remarkably heavy ; Mat, who was painting doors, com-
plained that she couldn't blow her nose, or light a cigarette
without getting paint on both.

Progress went to our heads. We scurried through our
meals and back to the job. I dug out the fungus that so
offended me, and cemented the hole, finishing it off with the
date and my initials. I used cement for purposes that even
a cement manufacturer has never suggested in his leaflets—
such as filling in the worn holes at the bottom of the door
planks.

We worked as furiously as if we had only the day in which
to finish. Our only breaks came when we went to the
waterfall for another ewer of water, and sat on the stone
step beside it for a few moments, to look at the mountains
and listen to the sounds—and then back again to walls and
doors. We kept saying, " Just this little corner here, and
then we'll stop," but somehow, when I had nearly finished
the corner, I would find I needed a little more cement, and
anxious not to mix *too* little and have to begin again, I would
mix too much. I couldn't contemplate wasting such hardly
won stuff, so then I had to start another hole to use it up.
The new hole would need more than I had and the whole
cycle began again. And Mat would say :

" It's a pity to leave this side half painted—the join might
show to-morrow," and having finished it and finding me still
at work, she would start the next board. So it went on ;
we were constantly overlapping our times and never managing
to finish together.

Eventually Mat said firmly :

" At half-past eight, whatever is unfinished, we stop."

With relief, I laid aside the board, and we had tea, so tired that we left the washing up, feeling it might be one of those times when cup handles come off, and plates slip out of the tea-towel.

Milk had to be fetched, and the dogs circumvented. Among them was a very short-legged terrier on a long elongated body—almost dachshund-like in her cut. She terrorized us for months. Her purpose was to harry out the foxes from their lairs during a foxhunt. Her low build enabled her to penetrate where others would jam, but her low intelligence never taught her to distinguish between us and foxes. Her name was " Nettle ", and as time went on she bore an amazing number of smaller nettles, each equally virulent, each bearing the same appropriate name. She was so very quick and nimble, and would be in with her nip and away, with a wide grin stretched over her nasty little yellow teeth before one knew she was there, for her size gave her the advantage of being able to creep under cover of the undergrowth. But for the fact that she wore her neck hair " en brosse " she could hardly be seen. Willie's grave, but not unsympathetic comment on her first bite was, " Ah yes, she is a very good hunter ! "

These were not ordinary dogs at all ; their personalities had no vulnerable spots through which one might make friendly contact. They were as hostile at the end as they were at the beginning of a holiday. As soon as we came within sight of the house, one of them would point his nose skywards, and give warning with a high, hysterical shout. From nowhere, his fellows would bear down in an alarmingly long, single file, leaping, yelling, and making wide detours to sneak up with our calves. Wellingtons were some defence, but who wants to wear Wellingtons on a hot summer evening ?

As we walked down that evening, we found we had developed a kind of occupational disease. Mat found she could not pass any tree without calculating how long it would take to paint its trunk, and I was mentally flicking cement into the thousands of holes in the dry stone walling as we passed by.

Coming home after the usual dog-skirmish, we discussed

having a day off from cement and paint. There were plenty of other jobs to be tackled as a change. We walked slowly up the fields. The sheep were settling down by the barn for the night. They were ceasing to look all alike to me, and were beginning to have faces of their own. " Sheep have not really got silly faces," said Mat, as she stopped to look at them.

" No," I said. " Arrogant, conceited, contemptuous, dig- nified, but rarely silly, especially the rams." One very handsome ewe with deep brown-black fleece, had eyes that seemed almost golden. She looked more like a faun or a satyr. We christened her " Beelzebub." Except for her small white lamb, she was always alone. The lamb often slept between the holly tree and the wall. I leaned over quietly one day and picked him up, startling him so much that he could not bleat, and was surprised to find that his little curls, looking so soft, were harsh and wiry to the touch. From noticing this pair, conspicuous in any gathering, we found that sheep are creatures of habit, and have a regular grazing round. They would be in the little garden one day, two days absent on the mountain, and on the fourth day back in the garden.

We had supper and went upstairs, giving a last satisfied look at our handiwork. The bedroom was looking more elegant too, for we had a little oasis in the expanse of floor, a rug that Mat had designed and worked at for weeks. It was patterned with a map, of the kind called in atlases, " Bathy- Orographical," which means, as far as I can see, that land is shown in greens and browns, and the depth of the sea in blues.

Next morning as I swam up through those delicious moments when one is not quite asleep, but certainly far from awake, I began to be conscious of aching arms, and then, dimly remembering our arrangement of the evening before, I went to sleep again. We woke late to a dull, grey day, windless and with a sky so dark that one could hardly tell where sky ended and mountains began. The barometer, my birthday present from Mat, stood at the cryptic statement " More Wind." The import of these remarks on barometers eludes me. It had been still weather for the last few days. How then, could we have *more* wind until we had had *some* wind ? If the comparative, why not the superlative ? Why does there never occur the phrase " Most Wind " or more appropriately " Most Awful Wind " ? It occurred in reality often enough.

We approached the morning's work in a leisurely manner. Mat disposed of all the movable rubbish hidden in the nettles. The nettles themselves she slashed down with a murderous-looking implement like a sickle. It was hair-raising to watch. The blade had such a curve on it that I feared her more energetic strokes might reach round the back and cut her in two. After some near misses, she tried slashing it in the opposite direction. It then, although looking safer for her, appeared as though it might, if it slipped, spear me to the front door where I stood watching, and I went inside. I was relieved when the weapon was put back on the table in the Gladstone-Disraeli room. Slashing the nettles was, we knew, only a half measure. But now their heads were off, one's eyes were not affected by their rank luxuriousness, and it was nice to walk by without seeing all the rusty iron and broken pots.

I began to put up a coat rack on the hall wall. It presented a smooth unbroken surface for my plugging, and taking the hammer and the Rawlplug tool, I marked two holes at the points where I had decided the rack should be screwed. Holding it in place, I called in Mat in order that she could say how nice it would look, and then began. The diagrams in the leaflet showed neat little holes with clean and well-defined circular edges. At my first blow, three cracks ran along the plaster, and about five inches of the surface split away and fell off. This was not shown in the diagram. I gave the tool another blow and down came the next layer. Pieces of plaster, as they drop, have an irrevocable sound. Like cups, as they fall, nothing can be done about them.

I withdrew the tool to look for the tidy, circular little holes which I feared would not be there. They were not. There was instead, a big, jagged hole into which I could have

emptied all my Rawlplugs, and then stuffed the cardboard
box on top of them. It looked bad, and I was anxious to
have it covered up before Mat came in. I put the tool in
again, and struck, but worse than the ugly hole—there now
came the new and final sound of metal striking on very hard,
immovable stone. The hole was not deep enough, and it
would go no further without blasting.

Under these smooth plaster walls, I had not imagined
I should meet unyielding rocks, but now I thought about it,
it was obvious that it was mainly what I should meet. How
then, was I to know where I could get a plug between the
unseen joints? In the dairy I found a metal skewer, and
using this as a probe, took careful soundings every few
inches, driving it through the plaster as far as it would go.
It was plain that a little Rawlplug was going to be no use
in holes of the magnitude I was making, and as soon as I
found a place where I could sink it up to the neck, I enlarged
it to take a big, wooden, home-made plug. It was much
more satisfactory making big bold holes than trying to make
small neat circular ones. There was a pleasant kind of
abandon about it. Small ones looked like a pinprick in
these vast areas. Into mine I could drive a plug about four
inches long, knowing it would be securely wedged between
two heavy stones. But now came a new problem—where
was the next hole to be found? The wall was not built
with even, regular joints such as occur in brickwork. My
coat rack was only four inches wide. Supposing there was
no other joint at the same level or even at three inches above
or below my first hole. Should I screw the coat rack on at
a slope, or should I have to knock holes all over the wall until
I discovered two at approximately the same level. I began
to wish I'd not thought of a coat rack, and certainly to wish
that I'd not invited Mat to see how nice it would look.

Taking the skewer, I made three more soundings. There
was the same unyielding ring of metal on stone.

I tried a fourth a little higher with the same result. The
rack was only five feet long. A plug further away than
three and a half feet was going to be no use. I tried the
next one a little lower, and to my relief the skewer went in

deep. Quickly, I made the hole and drove in a plug, and although the two were not on the same level, it was possible to screw on the rack so that it would hang straight. Soon, it was firmly on the wall, and where the experimental holes showed, I filled them with plaster of Paris mixed hurriedly in a cup. A quick scurry round to find clothes to hang on the pegs, and the job was ready for inspection.

In the dairy, I put up shelves, but I could see the joints, and there was no need for blind probings through plaster. It was rather a wasted effort to put one over the dairy table, as we carelessly charred most of it away that evening through leaving the lamp burning beneath it.

Inspired by the shelves bearing tins, jars and pans, Mat, who began to feel we had a modern labour-saving kitchen, made a cake and cooked it in the Rippingille oil-oven. We ate it, but obviously, oil-ovens were things one had to get used to, with quite different habits from gas-ovens.

It was an economical oven, for while one dish was cooking inside, little lids on top of the burners could be lifted off, so that pots could be boiling on top, too.

Mat's father had given us a very handsome model of a different type. It was an efficient cooker, but had, for me, one overwhelming drawback. One could see it consuming paraffin. It had a glass container for the oil, and every few seconds, a gurgling bubble rising to the top, showed that another drink had gone to the wicks. The frequency of the bubbles used to unnerve me. It reminded me so forcibly, that for every gulp I saw, that amount of paraffin would have to be carried three miles and more. I used to stand in fascinated silence, counting the bubbles, and reckoning their value in quarter pints. I grew ridiculously economical, and used to remove the meat under-done, and eventually became so alarmed at the rate at which fuel was consumed, that one day we gave up oil cooking altogether and tried the oven in the kitchen.

Mat lit the fire early one Sunday, pulling out various stiff and rusty dampers, and dislodging showers of soot. We had faith that the oven would get hot, for Enid, who so generously made most of our bread for the first few years, had told us that it cooked wonderful rice-puddings. At the time, our minds only registered the first half of her sentence, and it was only later that we remembered that rice-puddings are best in a slow oven.

After the fire had roared for nearly an hour, and the oven still remained cold, we raked about with the poker at the side of it, finding, to our satisfaction, a thick iron plate and two fire bricks, which we hooked out with tongs and shovel. With these out of the way, the fireplace was now gapingly large and hungrily asking for more. We pushed the red hot embers under the oven and piled more wood at the side. It was warming up, but slowly. We heaped on all the wood it would take, which happened to be all the wood we had, and went across the stream for more. Before we left, we put the small joint in the oven. We had not been fortunate with our joint that week, and it was a mere collection of bones held together by sinews.

We were absent for perhaps twenty minutes, but as we came in sight of the house, a faint blue haze was floating out through the open door. I had a sickening feeling that we had set the beam on fire, the lovely wide chimney beam that Mat had cleaned up to its pristine beauty. We dropped the wood and rushed in. The beam was still there, but even from the kitchen door we could feel the heat beating out of the oven, and could see the blue haze, faint no longer, but thick and smelly. With the tongs, we lifted the door on its broken hinge and retreated quickly from the heat. We went forward once more, and there in the oven lay our little joint ; a shrunken, blackened ruin. We replaced the iron plate and firebricks, and have cooked with oil ever since. What we lose on the swings we gain on the roundabouts. Paraffin has to be carried up, but there is less staggering through the bouldered wood and over the stream, bearing heavy oak boughs.

To improve the bedroom, we stained the floor. For this, we had meant to use Brunswick black and turpentine, but looking at the size of the floor, we felt that it would need too much. We tried a cheaper method recommended in the " Home Renovations " column of one of the penny dailies, which was to brush the floors over with a strong solution of permanganate of potash. It was an expensive experiment. Mat used our best distemper brush so as to cover the area quickly, leaving the space where the mattresses lay until later. For a day or two, other work was more pressing, and when we were ready to stain again, we found the hairs of the brush had prematurely withered, and fell away at a touch, leaving an almost bald stump of wooden head. We threw out the rest of the permanganate when we saw its effect on our best brush, and very soon had to throw out the brush too.

Knobs and locks were needed on doors and cupboards. I put two beechwood knobs on the kitchen cupboard and fitted a new panel in the broken half. To my eyes, it improved the kitchen enormously. It no longer looked so neglected. Jobs that one does one's self have that effect, I find, and for days they seem quite the most satisfactory thing in the room. As I sat at breakfast next day the cupboard door was reflected in the teapot, the new knobs appearing large and important in the curved shining surface of the china, the doors bulging above and below, and in the foreground a fat, smug, satisfied face, distorted like the startling images that confront one in the convex mirrors of fun-fairs.

The bottoms of the downstairs doors, where the hobnailed boots of generations had worn hollows in the threshold, needed door-sills, which we made from pieces of elm. They worked well as draught-excluders, and almost as well as death-traps. Many precipitate entrances were made by those who had not sufficiently heeded our warnings of " *Mind the step !* There is one at each door." And not only by others, for I remember Mat making a wonderful entry with a tray of crockery one morning. Realizing too late that she had forgotten to mind the step, she hurtled in, her head a foot ahead of her feet, arms and tray two feet ahead of either, and staggered straight towards the hearth, where I happened to be standing, looking with pleased satisfaction at some wooden brackets I had put above the door which were the apple of my eye at the moment. I was able to act as buffer.

THE HOUSE AND HOLLY WHEN WE FIRST TOOK IT

BLAEN Y CWM WITH EVENING SHADOWS ON THE GARN

Most of the crockery that fell off, fell on to the thick sheep-skin rug, and much of the rest happened to be odd plates.

About tea-time Willie arrived with horse and cart bringing the furniture. He sat on the wall and talked. Talk of cement and walls led him to talk of the high stone walls that ran across the face of the mountain, and of the men who had built them.

" A few pence a yard they had, and all the stone to carry. They were well made, but it was long ago, and they are falling in places. They will never be built again, for men will not climb these hills and work so now."

I asked him, but almost as a rhetorical question, where the sand was, and he slid off the wall and walked through the yard up the slope. There was a hole in the turf, about two yards wide.

" There, you see ! " he said, but I saw nothing but stony soil with a trickle of water running over it.

" I will show you. Have you a spade ? " He cut back the upper edge of the hole, and about a foot deep the earth began to look grey and fine. So it did exist ! We were as pleased as if he had discovered a stratum of gold-bearing rock.

" Does it go far ? "

" Very far, I think, for there is another small pit like this at the top of the hill, and you will get all the sand you need."

Twm, bored at lack of occupation, started to walk through a gap in the yard wall too small for the cart to follow.

"Hungry she is. There is the milking, too, and I must find the cows. I could not see them this morning," he added sadly, as he turned down the valley.

We filled several buckets, and tipped the sand into a heap to drain, ready for next morning, and as dark came, we went in.

Doors and windows were wide open as the atmosphere was so sultry. It was almost too hot to sleep, and the bleating of lambs sounded very loud in the quiet night. I did not seem to have been long asleep when Mat woke me.

" Listen ! " she whispered. There was no need to listen.

A strong wind had sprung up, and somewhere at the back of the house, I could hear a great clatter and jangle—an unexplainable noise we had never heard before. We sat up in bed, unable to ignore it, yet unwilling to investigate. The wind gathered again and roared up to a climax, dying away as it swept through the little wood, and leaving the air still and oppressive again. Only too willing to defer action until morning, I lay down and we exchanged theories. Perhaps a sheep had slipped in at dusk and was now knocking all the kitchenware on to the floor. It seemed possible. A ram had once jumped clean through the glass of Iolo's window and landed almost on his lap as he sat reading. We decided, not altogether convinced, that the sheep was a likely explanation ; we could leave it alone until daylight—it would teach it not to walk in through strange doors.

No sooner had we agreed on this, than there was a sudden hard slap at the wall behind us, as the wind beat at it again and passed down the valley. It seemed to suction the air from the room as it went and a quick, sultry puff came in to take its place. Once more it came, with such force that the room appeared to give a slight bounce. The noise below was alarmingly loud. It was impossible to think of sleeping. We decided we must go down. Stepping out on to the blue sea of the rug, I groped on hands and knees in the permanganate ocean to find the candle. We selected our weapons —an umbrella and a short length of coffin board.

Reluctantly, we opened the door and crept to the hall, and whilst we stood, gathering courage, the candle blew out as though someone had leaned over the stairs and puffed. We went back for matches—both of us—and down again. At the dairy door, with the clatter on the other side of it, my hair felt as though it was being stroked up from the back by some invisible hand. I turned the door knob. It was wrenched from me and flung against the wall as a gale swept through it into our faces as though we were on the open mountain.

As suddenly as before, it stopped, and with it the satellite janglings. We lit the candle again and looked fearfully about. Every tin, jar and saucepan we had that afternoon put on the shelves, was lying on the floor. Just above the window was a big black space in the plaster.

" It's the roof," said Mat. " There's a big hole in the corner." Slates lay smashed on the floor, and through the yard-wide gap, we could see a curiously luminous grey sky.

The wind dropped as suddenly as it had come, and the bleating of lambs came again on the still air. The rest of the night was quiet and hot again, although once I heard a long distant rumble of thunder, and until dawn there were intermittent flashes of lightning.

The repair of the hole was an important occasion, for after the new slates had been re-pegged, we cemented them all down, using sand from our own pit.

We had another shock next evening when we came back just after dusk with kindling fetched from the wood. As we dropped the bundles by the door, there was an odd scuffling noise and a dull bump at the other side of it. We hesitated, and went to peer through the kitchen window, and round to the open dairy window. There was nothing to be seen, and we slowly opened the door. Before it was a foot ajar, a black creature darted out, dashing between Mat's legs, and down the garden. It was a startling moment until we recognized the beast as the hearthrug dog. With the low cunning of its kind, it had leapt in at the open dairy window, eating to-morrow's dinner, which was lying on a tea-chest there, and wandered into the hall. A sudden draught must have slammed the dividing door and imprisoned it.

After this incident, I began to realize that I disliked coming into the house after dusk if windows or door had been left open. Often, in fine weather, we went out after the day's work to pick flowers, bathe in the pool, or gather kindling in the wood. Unless the door was shut, I always felt I must get home before the colours drained from the cwm and left it grey. It was not fear of Anything ; more a fear of Nothing. The door must be shut by dark ; which side of it we were was unimportant. I do not mind walking alone up the valley in any weather, at any time of night, or year, but to enter the house after dark, through a door that has been left open, needs all my courage. Why this should be, I do not know ; perhaps it has something to do with the spirit of the mountains, or perhaps it is something connected with the primeval fear of those great desolate places when daylight has gone from them.

The mountains are very beautiful, especially just before sundown when one sees them from the wood, and glimpses through the oak branches that last golden streak of light creeping to the summits. On days when the rain looks like a quickly moving curtain perpetually drawn across the valley, when water is pouring off every slope and the wind is tearing over their rocks, the mountains can be relentless. On a still day when the mist is thick and quiet, they can be baffling, for landmarks are hidden, and one walks, hoping that the familiar boulder, where one must turn, will soon appear, and fearing lest it does not. When they stand still and dark, they can be frightening. A place with such moods must surely have a spirit not to be found in more placid lowland country.

Sometimes, after a beautiful day, I have stayed too long in the upper cwm by the lake. I look up and the mountains seem to have stepped silently closer, and to be watching. Their feet have shuffled quietly nearer to the lake, the surface of the water has become dark and cold as they tower over it, and the great cwm has become grey and bleak and empty. Friendly rocks have lost their prominence, and have instead thrown in their lot and merged with the mountain. Everything is silently watching, and waiting for one to go—and to go quickly. When the cwm looks like that, it is no use reasoning about illogical fears. One goes—and one goes at once. Often I have rushed, stumbling over tussocks and rocks in the gloom, to get within the smell of my own wood fire, and the sight of my own roof before the mountains make the next step.

But what I expect to see on those evenings when I have left the door open, I never really know, unless it is the Spirit of the Cwm sitting in my armchair, waiting for me.

CHAPTER V

" I HAVE brought you a big watchdog," said Willie, with a grin. " With him on your doorstep, you will be very safe from burglars."

There he was—the bull who had lumbered towards us so purposefully on the day when we first saw the house. Transferred in summer to Blaen-y-cwm, for the greater safety of hikers, he lumbered purposefully about there too. It was no consolation to me that, if we were gored, we had been butchered to safeguard a hiker's holiday.

From now on, an interest in bulls was forced upon us : big bulls, little bulls, savage bulls, not quite so savage bulls, but all of them black-skinned and black-hearted bulls. Bulls kept us constantly exercised in mind and body.

In his youth, the Welsh bull is a podgy, square-headed calf with button horns, and a sulky appeal on his black face. One pats him as one would pat a large dog. Behind his black face his black mind is growing and, in some unfathomable way, his black thoughts are turning against the human race who so kindly bring him his buckets of food day after day. Suddenly, it is plain that his black heart has developed too. He has stopped being a calf, and has become a bull overnight. During that short period, his body has doubled, and his head quadrupled in size. It is the most extraordinary transformation I have witnessed, and when it has occurred, even allowing for my admittedly biased description of it, all relations, diplomatic and otherwise, are best severed.

He looks too clumsy to leap a wall. He is not. He is an agile beast, able to cross streams, leap walls, dodge round trees, and manœuvre his bulk neatly wherever it suits him.

This first one used to emerge from his field whenever it suited him, climbing out of it like something grown too big for its playpen, and, rolling across the fields switching his tail, dribbling, shaking his head, he would bring with him a cloud of large and most vicious looking flies. The cool shadows of the buildings used to call him at about eleven o'clock, and as they slipped round the house with the sun, he and the flies used to follow them. On such mornings, filling the water buckets was a hazardous business, and took our combined ingenuity. Hearing the door open, he might amble up to see what was afoot, but by the time he had arrived, the door was shut again, and the water-fetcher round the corner of the house, out of sight. The sound of the shut door always gave me a horrible sense of being alone in a wide world with a bull.

From the front windows, the look-out inside summed up the situation : was it safe to return via the door, or was it advisable to get through the dairy window ? And from the dairy window, the communiqué would be issued. As one waited, one faced towards the threatened danger. It was fortunate that he never seemed to realize that he could pull off a *coup d'état* by approaching from the back.

I was at the waterfall one day, waiting for the summary on the enemy position, when the dairy window burst open hurriedly.

" He's coming ! " hissed Mat.

" Take the bucket then," I said urgently, and prepared to flee round the back of the house. I swung it up, but it was too heavy, and while it still scrabbled precariously on the edge of the slate-sill, the familiar, ugly head appeared round the corner. Taking the bucket with me, I dashed round the back, clattered over the yard wall to the door, where there was a horrid wait of a second or two before Mat opened it, and I shot in, with a few inches of water covering the bottom of the four gallon bucket. Mat, for her part, wondered whether she would be opening the door to me or the bull. He came back and settled on the door-stones, and all afternoon we were passively besieged as he dozed, his huge forequarters jammed into the narrow opening. When the sun began to drop behind the oak wood, leaving the fields in a shadow that flowed to the base of the Garn and was beginning to spread up its slopes, he left us, returning to his playpen for the night.

Many were the new ways we evolved that year of dealing with the bull menace. The theory of taking the bull by the horns we turned down as just plain silly. It gave him a most unnecessary and undesirable advantage. When one has attached oneself to his horns, half his battle is over : he can toss or gore as his fancy dictates.

My father had always carried an umbrella when he walked through a bull field. He said—though whether he had ever had need to try it out I do not know—that if one faced the beast, and opened and shut the umbrella rapidly and repeatedly, it would puzzle him and he would go away. It was probably my father's wishful thinking, but it had certainly given him sufficient morale to walk into any field, and as we were in the state of mind to clutch at any straw, we used to walk down for the milk, still dressed in cement and paint-splashed clothes, carrying a large umbrella. These garments hardly looked the kind needing protection from sudden storms, so to avoid Willie's humorous comments, we left it hooked on the Canol gate, to pick up on the way back.

Fortunately, we never needed it : we never met him absolutely and unavoidably head-on, and he seemed happy enough to stay in his field at night.

As we neared the end of that first summer, most of the essential inside repairs were finished, though we could have continued for weeks filling up some of the more obvious mouse and rat entrances in the stonework at the back. The selection of the more deserving cases was difficult : there were so many holes from which to choose, and we could only afford time to attend to the more clamorous. Beyond the first few inches, it was impossible to gauge the spacious labyrinth to which the hole extended. I wished we could put them all in a riddle, and sieve them out in sizes, like potatoes, but we could only settle some sort of a precedence for them by holding a lighted candle at each, and assume the biggest draughts were those that blew out the light.

Decoration and repair improved the house enormously, though we became rather tired of the smell of paint and distemper, the blisters that came from putting them on, and the sameness of the occupation. It seemed never-ending, and the pool beneath the waterfall was rarely free of buckets and distemper brushes put there to wash overnight. The sudden discoloration of the clear water with diluted distemper as a brush was dropped in, always struck me as a sacrilegious act, as bad in its own small way as pouring millions of gallons of effluent into the Thames.

Practice had made us quite good at distempering, and we ceased to hear the patter of hundreds of little drops on the floor for each brushful that went on the wall, for we had at last mastered the unhelpful instructions on the tin—" Mix to the right consistency with a little water if necessary." As an example of futility, I always felt that this advice would be hard to equal. State the obvious ; ignore the essential. I suppose some people might try to mix it with milk or pale ale—I don't know—but the right consistency, what is it ? It would be simple enough to mix if one knew what it was, and the duty of the manufacturer seemed to me to be to describe it, and not just slip out from his obligations in that blatant manner.

We spent odd hours, as a change between one indoor job and another, in bringing in logs. It's an ill wind that blows nobody any good, and winter gales brought us much fuel. Scouring each wood in turn we searched for fallen branches. I trimmed up the main limbs, ready for sawing into manageable lengths, while Mat painstakingly scraped off moss and loose bark, for she loathed the insects and grubs they harboured. There were sickly looking fat, white things with brown heads and legs, and woodlice, centipedes and millipedes. The legged creatures were not as objectionable as the lifeless-looking white grubs and one could only imagine into what they would hatch. Imagination told Mat that they would grow into something the size of a white rat, with heads like the magnified pictures of a bluebottle's eye, and with a lot of brittle short legs that would enable the creatures to scamper out of sight when we appeared. The idea of a lurking army of such horrors in our woodpile revolted her, and every bit of rotting bark had to be scraped off before the logs came indoors.

Our methods of getting the lengths home differed. Mat preferred to hug one end of hers, and obstinately trail, tug and roll it over bogs and rocks. Crossing the stream, trailing was no use, nor were rolling and tugging, and here she gathered the whole of it to her bosom. The effort of carrying it and balancing on slippery stones was often too much, and they both fell in. I preferred to pad my shoulder and balance the burden there, walking as quickly as possible to the first resting place. We had recognized stopping places on every route—posting houses at which we often wished we could have had a change of horses too, for a short length of sound oak is surprisingly heavy. If it is not, it is rotten, and not worth the effort of carrying home.

Down the slope of the woods, we used to roll the logs, but when one end was thicker than the other, they would never roll straight, and we had to start them off on a new course every few seconds. When we had to bring them *along* the contours, we dragged them on a rope, but it was always as well to be on the top side of it, for if they started rolling, one had either to drop them, or be carried down too, and often, there was not even a choice. Up near the mountain wall we found a huge, fallen birch, and spent a few glorious hours bringing it down by the lumberjack method. Each piece was launched as it was cut, and all afternoon we splashed in and out of pools, often waist deep, prodding, pulling and pushing them along with a meat hook lashed to a six-foot length of ash. It was good fun, but saved no labour. The logs got jammed where the stream narrowed for waterfalls, they hid in the shadows of overhanging trees and pretended to be rocks, they slid out of sight under the banks, and at the end of the day when we counted them up, we had unaccountably lost two.

In Dolgelley, we bought an axe for splitting the bigger logs ; a lovely long-handled woodman's axe with a smooth, curving ash handle. I remembered how, as a small girl, I had watched with envy, a woodman splitting logs, and one day, when he was out of sight, had tried it myself, neatly chopping off the end of one toecap, and going to endless trouble to keep it from the eye of authority for a few days.

Use gave confidence, and log-splitting became pleasurable. Logs, laboriously sawn, quadrupled themselves and accumulated into a large pile in the chimney corner, a promise of crackling fires through the long, dark Christmas evenings. As well as the axe, we had a big two-handled saw and a smaller axe for the twiggy kindling. Carrying home these weapons had called forth many facetious comments, and Evan Jones, as we had passed his farm with them, had thrown back his head and roared with laughter.

" Travelling forestry workers ? " he said. " Put me down for two tons. Coal will be short this winter."

It struck me one wet day that I might invent a speedier way of getting our logs home—in loads instead of singly. The first experiment towards this end was a sled, and to explain what now seems a curious choice, I should make it clear that there were so many sleds in our valley, that I felt they must have some particular, though not very obvious advantage not possessed by a wheeled vehicle. All the farmers used sleds for haymaking on their sloping fields. They were much heavier and more cumbersome than ours, being made from thick lengths of split oak. One often met them, pulled easily along the steep fields by a horse. It didn't strike me when I was making ours that we were not horses, and after valiant and muscle-straining efforts, during which it had every opportunity to prove its value and failed, we decided that sleds are used mainly because they can be made at home, have no expensive wheels, need no brakes on the gradients, being extremely efficient brakes in themselves, and because one's horse, having known nothing better, does not complain.

Before dragging up coal from the other side of the bridge— where everything was dumped as being the outermost fringe of civilization, we tried our sled out on the logs. In a flush of enthusiasm I visualized one or two trips to the wood, returning piled high with fuel. No more of those endless trips, struggling with a single refractory length of oak bough. The work of log collecting, I fondly imagined, would be reduced by three quarters.

Up to the top of the little wood behind the house we went,

tugging the sled. It was easy enough over the short, dry, slippery grass. At the top of the wood, we loaded up six thick sections of fallen tree—a morning's work to get them home, carried in our usual fashion. Lashing them on with a series of elaborate and efficient looking knots, we turned the nose for home, and putting ourselves inside the loop of rope, we started. Down the slippery slope we went, first at a walk, then at a trot, and finally at a gallop, the sled slithering after us. Once the heavy mass had started to move, there was no means of slowing it, and our anxiety was to keep our heels from being overtaken. The performance became a vicious circle ; we speeded up to avoid the lumbering load ; it, unable to do otherwise, followed suit, and as the danger of losing our heels grew more imminent, we sped faster. Our fate was tied up for better or worse, with the stout hempen rope and the burden following us. As we all galloped down the slope, retribution joined in and galloped too. Near the bottom, it overtook us, and a terriffic and breathtaking tug on the rope seemed almost to cut my waist in two. I looked quickly down to see how far I had been severed, and finding myself still whole, collapsed on to the grass to recover my wind. Breath returned, and we got up to find the reason for the disaster.

" Girling brakes," said Mat, as she saw the projecting stump that had halted us, " have nothing on a sled. Stop in your own length."

We started again, choosing the route carefully, and walking. As we crossed the bog, the drawbacks of a sled became plain. I saw in my mind, those pictures, beloved of calendar makers, of timber hauliers with a pair of Clydesdales straining every muscle to tug a timber waggon through a slough of mud. Except that we pawed with our front feet in the air, the action was, on a smaller scale, equally vigorous. We threw off two logs and tried again. At the gateway we jettisoned two more, and before we reached home we were pulling an empty sled. For three days, logs lay strewn along the route we had taken ; a monument to a painful failure, and then we went out and brought them in in the old slow, laborious way.

As a result of using our petrol to fetch sand, we set out on foot a day or two later, to find the way over the mountain to the village shop ; the post office, where groceries, picture postcards, hardware, mending wools, brooms, lemonade, fish hooks and bootlaces were combined in one magnificent collection under the same roof.

Enid, we knew, went by a short route of about three miles. After the evening milking, she would often what she called " run over " for four ounces of yeast for next day's baking. All we had to do, was to run over too, and then walk leisurely back with our shopping. But of course, one run might be more strategic than another, and we called on Willie to discover the best.

" You go past the ruined building beyond the corner of my house, over the field, across the old tramway from the goldmines and on towards the wood. You must not stay by the wood for long," he added mysteriously. The danger, we gathered, was not so much the being in the wood, as being unable to get out of it. Unfortunately, once in, we were in for a very long time. The going was rough, for it lay on a steep part of the mountain, and the rocks littering it were of a huge size. Most of the time we zig-zagged about, avoiding some, clambering over others, working round fallen trunks, but finding no track. I began to feel, in the directionless scurrying, rather like an ant. We reached the top corner at last, hot, sticky, and bitten by stinging insects.

Climbing the rickety wall, we were relieved to find ourselves out of the wood, though, in another sense, still very much in it, for beyond the wood stretched a sea of the tallest bracken I have ever seen. It was well above neck height, and often, over eye level. Walking in it was as baffling as walking in a thick fog. We were constantly sweeping it apart to try to get some idea of our whereabouts, and all that appeared were the tops of more bracken beyond. I know nothing more tiring than wading through bracken—a frustrating, hemmed-in kind of occupation. For almost an hour we fought upwards, seeing nothing but bracken fronds and sky.

It was plain that we had stayed in the wood much too

long, and emerged from it at the wrong place. "Let's give it up and go back," I said. "It's much too exhausting on a hot day." We sat down to smoke a cigarette and keep the flies at bay, and heard, in the silence, a few yards above us, the slight, pattering noise of sheeps' hooves on rock. Since leaving the wood we had seen no rock at all. We got up and pushed through the bracken towards the sound, and there two yards from where we sat, was the track, a string of sheep trotting down it parallel to the route up which we had struggled. It was very galling. But having stumbled on it, we felt we might as well use it. In a series of ups and downs, it reached the shoulder, descended a steep slope to the next valley, and in course of time brought us to the post office. Our shopping list had been reasonably small when we began, but it was a fascinating shop, and when we left, our packs bulged. Halfway up the long slope home, Mat produced from the back pocket of hers, a large bottle labelled, "All Fours Cough Mixture."

"It's all I can offer you, I'm afraid," she said gravely. "Let's try it."

At each gate, we had another dose, and it provided a little stimulus to us as our steps grew slower and slower. By the time we were in sight of our house, the bottle was empty, and as I flung it to the rubbish heap, I noticed on its label, "It is dangerous to exceed the stated dose."

We turned our attention to other additions, and made birch brooms with hazel stick handles, so that we could sweep the stone slabs to the waterfall, and an uncouth-looking rake with split oak teeth to rake up nettles and bracken. We acquired an old scythe, and when I was able to prevent the point from digging itself into the earth, I was able to wreak a wide devastation in a short time. From the heaviest of the logs, I fashioned a beetle, in case, when we next needed it, the one by the shed had gone. A contraption of wires, bent at right angles and spliced to a long handle, worked admirably for clearing weeds from the source of our water supply. It must have been the finest collection of primitive farm implements existing, outside a museum.

I took to pieces the "Whirlwind" carpet sweeper picked

up in a sale, and made it whirl beautifully, but it was love's labour lost, for on our uneven floors, its mouth was either wheezing hungrily three inches above the carpet, or jamming tightly on it and suffocating itself.

To store the paraffin which we brought up by the gallon each time we went down the valley, I soldered a tap into an empty five gallon oil drum.   At two o'clock one afternoon, I took a pound of solder, and by tea-time I had used it all, and produced a curiously shaped excrescence on the drum, with the tap leaning drunkenly from it.

I erected a rough bench in the back for odd jobs, and made a medicine chest.   Into it, we packed as many bandages, ointments, lotions, potions and elixirs as would supply a small Himalayan expedition.   Among the potions was another bottle of " All Fours."

The hot, blue flames of the Primuses had become a smoking, sluggish yellow, and we bought spare parts and overhauled them.   Testing one, I forgot to replace the baffle cap first, and a searing, hissing flame shot into the air, singeing off Mat's eyebrows and some of her front hair.   Fortunately, she had a few weeks in which to grow a new crop before appearing in public.

We found that, as well as bulls, sheep went with the house, so to speak, in the manner of fixtures and fittings.   The bolder spirits would live inside with us, given half a chance.   They often walked in if the door was open, and sometimes, if we appeared suddenly, after a long quiet interval, the rug lying in the hall, got up, surprised, shook itself, and scampered out into the sunshine, leaving behind, for minutes after its departure, the strong, oily smell of sheep.

On summer nights, as the next best thing to living with us, they crowded, as many as could, to sleep on the cool stones outside the door.   As long as they slept quietly, they could be tolerated, but when the restless or cough-afflicted were among them, there was little sleep for us.   The sudden cough of a sheep in the night is enough to wake anyone : a tortured, human kind of sound, dry and rattling.   The merely restless are infuriating with their insistent bleating.   I endured one beneath the open window for an hour one night, and then in sudden fury, rushed downstairs and chased the whole flock, innocent and guilty alike, to the top wood, returning breathless in a still and moonlit world, with the dew cold on my feet.

In the early summer, they are gathered for washing, dipping and shearing, and as shouts, barks and whistles come nearer, a maze of thin trickles of sheep and lambs winds down the tortuous tracks, joining and thickening to a broad ribbon as they meet on the floor of the cwm. Urged on by shouts of men and barking of dogs, they scurry in a hot, excited mass, with a patter of many hoofs into the wide, green lane. If any late lambs have been gathered in, they are castrated with a shining instrument kept carefully wrapped in its box in the Gladstone-Disraeli room, and called, "The Bloodless Castrator." Those which have avoided being earmarked, either because they had evaded the last round-up, or because their mothers had missed the pre-natal coddling in the maternity field, and chosen independence and labour alone in some high and remote cwm, are earmarked and branded. Many of the lambs have quite lost their lamb look by the time they first meet *homo sapiens*.

Earmarking, unlike castration, has bloody results, though they often verge on the comic. A few drops of blood from the cut trickle down the lamb's face and become diffused on the damp wool, giving its features the appearance of a rouged and sophisticated old harridan's, and it is a colourful crowd when the dip has an orange tint and the greys of yesterday are replaced by striking and fashionable sunset shades for the adults.

Anxious mothers try to sort out their own offspring after the day's hurly-burly. The offspring will reject its shorn or dipped parent, now changed in smell, and be butted and angrily rejected itself by one it had thought its mother. Scampering up eagerly for a long-awaited drink, it may be refused in great indignation, and will trot about the flock, confused and bewildered, like a lost and frightened child, bleating hopefully at every new face.

Peace follows chaos, and relationships are sorted out. Reunited families recede from sight up the tracks down which the grey ribbons had trickled, and the ascending stream of the shorn or dipped is followed by happy, skipping little lambs on their way back to the high cwms.

One exciting morning, we assisted, or at least, were present at, a mass rescue. On the skyline by Craig-y-Deryn, a little waterfall tumbles over the rocks. Its position is so exposed that, when the wind is strong, it rises, blowing high into the air as fine spray. I first noticed it one very wet day, billowing into the sky like smoke, and went excitedly to tell Mat that the mountain was on fire, though it did occur to me that it was strange that it should flourish in such a downpour. We climbed up towards the crag to put it out, and save the rest of Merionethshire from conflagration.

Since then, we have seen Richard Jones looking like an incendiarist as he walks the mountains with a flaming torch to fire the old heather. If we saw the mountain on fire now, we should let well alone.

Up at the top, we found, not smoke, but spray blown back twenty yards, to fall and pour again in a stream to the edge of the cliff, in a vain attempt to fulfil its nature and fall. " Even the weariest river winds somewhere safe to sea." When the wind is strong, it must take this one a very long time. On the way back, we saw the sheep—ten of them on a high ledge from which there seemed no escape. They huddled together, quiet and miserable, and we, proud of ourselves in the rôle of rescuers of the benighted, went off to inform Richard Jones. But Richard Jones already knew. I think he is aware of how each individual sheep spends every hour of its waking day, and he can certainly recognize any of his flock without needing to see earmark or branding. At Christmas, we gave him a photograph I had taken of them, crowded together in the green lane. He had it framed, and can recognize each one like a near relation.

" This is the bad old ewe that jumps all the walls," says he, pointing, " and there is the lamb that came very late and we did not find until July."

For three days, he waited to see whether the stranded sheep would find a way back up the steep jump, and each morning, we anxiously scanned the ledge through binoculars,

Table and Dining Chairs; Three-legged Stool beyond

From the Front Door

to be sure none was dying from starvation, giving them another look over before night blotted them out again. By Sunday, he judged they were sufficiently exhausted to be apathetic and came up, bringing Willie, a neighbour, and the dogs— all of them ; there seemed to be more dogs than sheep. We went too, taking (at Willie's request) our climbing rope.

" They will be weak now," said Richard Jones, as we reached the crag, " and tired, so that when we get on to the ledge they will not leap off in fear. If we had gone to them the first day, they would have jumped over and perhaps killed themselves." And to Willie—" Get the rope thrown over the old rowan tree up there if you can, and we will climb up."

Willie flung it craigwards ; it went neatly over the tree, and he anchored it securely. Three of us clambered up, and with us, somehow or other, came a couple of dogs who, with military discipline, lay down immediately to keep the sheep cornered.

There followed a most amazing and alarming sight : of sheep seized, bundled up, and one after the other, slid over the edge of the forty foot cliff to land on the rough scree below. Some turned one somersault, some two or three, but every one of those bundles of wool arrived the right way up on its four sticks of legs, shook itself, and after a startled look round, hobbled off down the slope. No pro-longed rest in hospital after suffering exposure, starvation and shock.

The early humiliation of not being able to find the way out of our own valley sent us, as soon as possible after our return home to buy four sheets of six-inch map. After some trouble, we managed to get them at Stanfords, for at that time one had to produce a good reason for wanting a six-inch map ; and when the assistant had spread them on the counter, we explained that we wanted to find the best way of reaching this set of black dots from that set of black dots. It convinced him apparently as a reason as good as any other and we took the four home. When we laid them out on the floor, we were stunned by the multiplicity of tracks marked on that mountainside. Many of them seem to have disappeared since the area was mapped. Thinking it over, I decided that perhaps the cartographers also had fought their way out of that sea of bracken, and going angrily home, drew in a number of haphazard dotted lines where they felt tracks ought to be.

CHAPTER VI

THE days of holiday grew fewer and fewer, the last day came, and we returned home. We had a fairly clear idea of what we still needed, and foremost in my mind was the idea of a little cart. The six mile journeys to station and post office took a good deal of time, expecially when we had to make two trips because we couldn't carry everything in one. It seemed to me, that one journey on wheels by road, would be quicker than those eternal " runs " over the mountain with rucksacks.

In a junkyard we got a pair of carrier cycle wheels, the blacksmith made an axle so that I could bolt the body to it, and I set to work on the coachwork. It was in elm, of course, strong but not heavy, for we were to provide the motive power. Two stout screw eyes on the front allowed a length of rope to be attached for an extra puller, for any stray walker might offer his help, and it would be a bitter thing to have to refuse because there was nowhere he could lay his hand. When it was finished Ruth suggested we called in the local signwriter and had our names and address painted on it. I tried it out along the Banbury road one evening after blackout time. Mat came with me, but refused to act as cargo and sit in it so that all we discovered from the trial trip was that it ran easily and felt reasonably light, though later, when pulling it up the bog, it seemed to have lost both these qualities.

One September morning, we started early for Oxford, and on the road just outside the village found a dead badger. He was still warm, and had obviously been struck by some passing vehicle, although unmarked by the impact. We began to lift him into the ditch, when Ruth stroking his white striped face said, " Wouldn't he make a lovely hearth-rug ? " We looked at him, he certainly was attractive. Perhaps the village odd-jobs man would skin him. It seemed an idea worth considering, and we lifted him into the boot. He was so big that the boot would not shut, and we were compelled to park the car in Oxford with a dead badger in full view.

When we got back, I went to find Henry, but he was in bed with lumbago. His wife seemed to think it was rather a peculiar job we were offering, and dubiously said he'd come down if he felt better. From her tone, I gathered that it was not likely, if she had anything to do with it. Two days went by and no Henry appeared. We began to wonder what to do with the body in the coalshed, for it was plain that Henry's wife had no intention of letting him come.

" Skin him yourselves," said Ruth. " It can't be much different from a rabbit."

" Shall we ? " said I to Mat.

" We might," said she, dubiously.

That night, we skinned him, by the light streaming from the kitchen light into the garden. It was a horrible job. He smelt, he was unpleasantly greasy, and his skin stuck to him more tightly than any rabbits.

" It's just struck me why it's so nasty," said Mat, half-way through the job, " All the rabbits we've skinned have always had their insides taken out before we get them."

When at last it was done, we went in and had a brandy, then nailed the skin to a board to dry, covered with salt and a sprinkling of alum. The worst part was still to come, and that was—how to dispose of the body. Like murderers, once embarked, we had to get rid of the corpse.

We ran an allotment on what had seemed to be, as we dug it, virgin ground, hitherto untouched by hand. It produced in fullness of time, blowsy cabbages and woody radishes. Here we decided to bury him—darkly and at dead of night.

The following dinner-hour we dug a deep hole among the cabbages, watched by curious eyes from behind the windows of the nearby house.

As soon as dark came, we put him in the barrow, and pushed it out into the road. After a few steps we took him back again because the barrow was too noisy, and this was a clandestine sort of job. I got out the cart with its pneumatic

tyres and silent bearings, and covered the bottom thickly
with newspaper. Silently skirting the wall of the churchyard,
we reached the allotment by a devious route. The badger
smelt badly now, and I hoped the sack he was in would be
strong enough to hold him as we lifted him over the wall,
for I could not bear to touch him again. The window was
dark behind its blackout, and we made no sound as we
dropped him on to the soft earth and quietly scrambled after
him, but we couldn't find his grave. We crawled all over
the allotment on hands and knees, afraid that if we walked
upright, we should find it too suddenly. When at last we
had found the hole, we had lost the body, and Mat stayed
by the hole while I went groping back to the wall. Feeling
my way along, I came across him, mostly by smell, and
dragged him along, deciding that if the sack gave way, I
should just desert the job. But it held, and we rolled him
in his shroud into the grave, and pushed the earth quickly
over him, wondering whether the inquisitive watcher of the
afternoon would, when she saw the hole filled in, dig it up,
and inform Scotland Yard. We uprooted a cabbage to
plant over him, so that she would be deluded and try somewhere else for the hole.

Walking home, Mat quoted,

> " I sometimes think that never blows so red
>   The rose as where some buried Cæsar bled ; "

and had fantastic ideas of the cabbage shooting up in the
night like Jack's beanstalk.

Nothing much ever came of the skin. It dried stiff and
board-like, and we put it away in a corner of the cycle shed.
Mat suggested that we made it into shaving brushes, but
none of us needed a shaving brush, and when we took it
out, months later, the moths had got into it and eaten away
its face markings. On the way to Banbury one day, we
threw it over a hedge, and there, as the fairy tales say, it may
still be to this day.

We had a kind of Gallup poll on the most desirable piece
of furniture to make next. General opinion said that it

should be something *firm* to sit on, for the extraordinary unevenness of the kitchen floor, where there was, literally, no spot where all four feet of any article could be on the floor together, had caused such wear and tear that the stools were in danger of falling to pieces.

At first, we thought of tiling the kitchen floor, but it would have been such an expensive job that it seemed easier to do something about the furniture. I entered the three-legged era, for one could put down three legs firmly without the numerous exploratory proddings of the carpet to discover the deeper hollows. The three-legged solution took a firm hold of my imagination and everything that I could make this way, I did, beginning (after the new stools with three splayed legs) with a rough copy of the round table in the Gladstone-Disraeli room. Three-legged tables are rather common in Wales. Can it be that all Welsh houses had uneven floors ?

Working on this table set, for me, complicated mathematical problems. I found at last a practical use for Euclid, and settled down to study all the theorems concerned with triangles, for the table had no easy right angles in it anywhere, and when I had planned it, I drew it. It looked quite a reasonable kind of shape, so, trusting to Euclid to have been correct in his deductions, I embarked. Taking my courage in my saw hand, I cut, and was very relieved when it began to look more or less like the drawing. We rubbed the top with linseed oil, and put it all aside to await the next consignment. As the war went on, times taken in transit grew more and more erratic. One package took seven weeks ; another, sent rather late, seemed to arrive by air mail. The railway had hundreds of different kinds of charges too, according to how one described the contents, and we used much ingenuity in choosing a heading which allowed it to travel cheaply while still keeping within the bounds of truth. I thought several times of suggesting to the G.W.R. that they extend their passenger classes into the realm of goods travel, with say, an extra fourth class added for parcels willing to travel in open trucks and, during the summer, excursions or cheap day fares, with reductions for other members of the same family such as small stools not yet fourteen years of age, and for articles that could nestle into a larger one—free travel as for a child in arms.

The three-legged table now stands in a corner of the hall, and is very handy for holding whatever one happens to have brought up the valley on a dark night : milk can, groceries, keys. With encumbrances dumped on the table, one is then free to fumble about for lamps, fall over door sills, or sink into the floor depressions without fearing that one has kicked over the milk too.

I now got a kind of fever of work, and decided I could furnish the whole house. I started on a colossal piece—a hall seat that would take four people. The sides were shaped with a bow-saw from elm eighteen inches wide. The curves swept outwards half-way from the top so as to form the arms. Oh, the creeping progress of a bow-saw in hardwood one and a half inches thick, and the terrible boredom of the sawyer ! Hour after hour, on goes doggedly one, and at the end of the evening's work, no achievement beyond the curved cut, perhaps two feet long.

A pair of bellows followed. I took the cottage pair to pieces to see how they were made, and scoured the hedges for the willow wands which give the leather bellows their shape. The blacksmith made the nozzle for me. They turned out to have wonderful lungs, and though they were rarely needed for the fire, which roars up the chimney as soon as a match is put to it (except on the day we arrive), they have been a godsend for blowing off the sooty hangings from the inside of the oil oven, at those disastrous times when we have forgotten about it, and gone into the dairy to find smoked black festoons hanging everywhere, and little black, tadpole-like shapes resembling liver spots, floating in the atmosphere.

Again came the dreary and laborious business of the bow-saw—when I made two dining chairs. Bow-saws always seem so blunt too. Eight curved cuts had to be made, in timber an inch thick and three feet long. After cutting the first leg, I prayed heaven either to warp the rest of them to the correct curve during the night, or to send me a small power-driven saw. After cutting the second, I decided to get one for myself, and went to look at such things and find their prices. While pondering on their prohibitive expense, and wondering how many years it would take to raise the money in threepenny bits, I absent-mindedly cut the third, and then, having managed three, I somehow managed the fourth.

A few weeks later, I discovered that my timber yard would cut curves. My feelings were divided between joy and savagery. Why had they not announced the fact in neon lights on their signboard? Why was there no indication of this sideline on their billhead? Why could they not have simply said to me " We cut curves " ? Meanwhile I had already started on a pair of arm-chairs with nothing but straight lines in their make-up. They had long low seats so that one could lounge in them. As Mat said :

" Another of these seats where we sit on the floor ! "

When the frames were finished, they looked like some sort of patent cage in which to keep an animal, but we optimisti-cally bought a book on upholstering, and savage looking curved needles, twine, hessian, kapok and gaudy webbing. Springs or hair it seemed impossible to buy—they were scarce, and every upholsterer wanted them for his own work. After weeks of frustration, Mat had the masterly idea of going to car breaker's yards, and buying old car seats. We ripped them up and delightedly tore out the big copper springs and piles of hair, which we washed and put on the lawn in heaps to dry.

Next evening Mat came in, bringing the framework of one of the chairs, the instruction book, and trailing yards of twine up the stairs. We looked at the pictures, which were rather thick and smudgily drawn. The springs in them looked tied down in every possible direction. The idea impressed itself on our minds, that springs for some reason, must be firmly leashed, and anxious to do the thing properly we compressed ours very firmly indeed before they were secured. It struck neither of us that the whole point of a spring is to spring. While I held them, Mat anchored them firmly down with the best and strongest upholsterer's twine. It was a bad mistake, but they were bad drawings. When the backs and seats had been covered in pleasant green hessian to match the dining chairs, we tried them. The sitting *angle* was comfortable enough, but the sitting *surface* was excruciating ! The compressed springs lay very near the top, and sitting on them I felt as I imagine it would feel like to sit on those two very knobbly looking bones in the back of a cow, and there was nothing for it but to rip it all out and start again.

As a rest, I changed over to working in softwood, and made the rest of the things for the dairy, and these Mat painted white so as to make the rather dilapidated place look brighter.

" I always forget that things with four legs have sixteen sides," sighed she next evening as she saw several unpainted sides staring at her. " Well—I'll put that right, and then I might as well give the rest its second coat."

" Which had one, and which two coats ? " she muttered next day. " Never mind. I'll just paint where it seems to need it." Next time she saw it, she gazed at it with a depressed expression.

" A lot more places seem to need it now," she said, " and when they are dry, I expect there will be a lot more. This job is going to hang about for days."

I turned my attention to handyman's requisites ; a saw horse because our main fuel supply (apart from a little coal) was to be, not peat as Mat had hopefully thought—the old peat beds needed too much clearing—but the branches and logs we had collected. Remembering Mat's early struggles in scraping beams from a farm ladder, I made, too, a double sided step-ladder, and hinged the two sections so that it could be used also, in one length, as a ladder. But I overlooked one thing. When stretched out like this, the steps on one section sloped properly, but those on the other side were inside out, so to speak, and I could only stand uncomfortably on the narrow edge, with toes and ankles stretched and downward pointing, like those of an extremely clumsy ballet dancer. With practice, one could take a quick run up the first five awkward steps, and land in safety and comfort on the other half with its properly lying steps, but later I had to think out a way of altering them.

Then came a coal box, with wrought iron handle and fittings from the blacksmith. Remembering the size of the kitchen grate, I felt I must make it large enough, but alas ! the size I made it, when filled with coal, was too heavy to lift. So we simply kept it by the grate, filling it up from buckets when it got empty.

By this time, my unconscious slogan must have been on the lines of the florist's " Say it with flowers." Mine was— " Make it in wood." I made an oak kettle lid to fit a large, lidless iron kettle we had furtively snatched from the Dolgelley junk heap. It has grown very black with smoke, but has not, as one might imagine, gone up in it.

By this time we had enough furniture for the ground floor of the house. There were the hall seat and table, the dairy furniture, and in the kitchen was a big table, a small one, two dining chairs, two arm-chairs, coal box, bellows, kerb, bookshelves and stools. I turned my attention to upstairs.

Mat now had a bed there, and I had an old camp bed which really belonged to the cottage in Oxfordshire. We needed another bed, a chest of drawers, a bedside table, a chest for blankets and a wardrobe.

The timber would cost a fortune nowadays, but soaring costs had not really got under way, and looking through old bills, before throwing them out recently, I worked out that the elm for the two dining chairs had cost four shillings.

The bedroom furniture was big, and was going to need much labour to plane by hand. But my discovery that I could have curves cut had led to further exploration. I found something even more useful than curves, for walking through the timber merchant's extensive yard one day, I heard one of those vibrating, machine noises that seem to go with timber yards, and saw, in a long open shed, a sort of snow shower of shavings and chips whirling up from a heavy substantial-looking piece of machinery. Going up closer, I saw that it was actually planing. I watched it, thinking of my twenty-four inch plane and the energy I had put into it—and then I thought of a wardrobe six feet high and three feet deep, with huge double doors ; so massive that we could store mattresses in it to be safe from mice when we went away, and my heart lifted. With a leviathan of this kind to do the hard work, I could afford to use my energy in less utilitarian ways. I could spend some time on the arts and graces of woodworking. I could decorate it.

I started the bed ends, with raised panels—raised by gouging the surround from the rectangular centre. I liked the angled cuts it left, like adze work on old beams. The wood—Dutch elm—had two beautiful green streaks running through it. It was satisfying to be able to afford the time to decorate it—not very much ; the legs stop-chamfered, and the framework of the panelling also. We found metal supports to take the wire mattress which Mat had found in the loft at home in London.

Then came the chest with five drawers. The drawer fronts had a lovely twisting grain : it gave me great pleasure to run my hands over it and follow the swirls and turns. I spent a long time polishing it and fitting it with curved elm handles, and after this preliminary practice I felt able to tackle the wardrobe. The carcase was of great wide planks ; the widest I had used, and it had two compartments. The right hand side shelves could be slipped out to make storage room, and the other side had an extending rail for garments on clothes hangers. The double doors, with four panels in each, were finished like those of the bed. Even when it was packed flat, its railway ticket was costly.

Finally came the blanket chest made to match the rest. The lid shut with a heavy medieval sound, and the key turned in the lock with a loud and final-sounding click.

The chest stands against the yellow walls, and the sun, near midday, catches the top of the lid and shines across the many-angled cuts. Of the houseful of converted coffin boards, it is my favourite piece. When, on a wet day, I decide to polish the furniture, it is always the chest on which I begin, for I know I shall give up polishing before I have got as far as the large areas of the wardrobe, and by beginning here I am assured the chest gets its quota, whatever else is missed.

In case we ran out of paraffin and had to rely on candles for our lighting, I made a wooden chandelier for Blaen-y-cwm kitchen. It was wheel shaped with flat spokes, but had so many pieces that it needed all three of us to assemble it, for as soon as one piece fitted, another piece came out. We pushed and we panted and we struggled, and for a long time for each step forward there seemed to be two steps back. It must have looked like some strange ritual. In the centre of the floor was a wheel, and around it knelt three people with bowed heads and clenched teeth, speaking no word, but pushing, in a tense and dogged silence. It took almost an hour to get those eight little joints into place, and properly tightened up.

The timber merchant made eight small bowls of elm on the lathe, and to fit into these I bought eight brass candle sockets. I like the ironmongers of country towns. They can produce whatever you want from the dusty cardboard boxes stored on their topmost shelves. We bought a dozen green candles, and on Mat's birthday it was finished. We hung it from the ceiling beams by a wrought iron chain, and on festive occasions we turn out the Tilleys, light the eight candles, and sit in semi-gloom.

CHAPTER VII

SOON after this, Mat was recalled to London to take a job in a boys' school. The Sunday of that week we got out the Morris, and loaded it up in a depressed silence.

Whenever she could, she returned for a week-end, bringing various articles to add to the stores, and at Christmas we started for Wales again.

It was a bitterly cold evening. As I drew water from the well for the radiator, my hands froze to the well chain, the sort of experience I had read about in stories of Polar exploration, though not in connection with well-chains. Thick hoar-frost covered the trees and grass, and the road sparkled treacherously in the headlights. We started from Oxfordshire with hot-water bottles at boiling point, but they were cold in an hour or so. The chill air penetrated the thickest clothing and my feet were numb and leaden. At Wellington, fine powdery snow began to fall. The windscreen wipers pushed a little wedge of it to and fro—always, when it was just on the point of falling, the other wiper would take it up and slide it neatly to its mate—shaping the edges between them like a pair of butter pats. The air stabbed in keen, sharp spears through the gaps in sidescreens and footboards. It was Mat's turn to sleep, and I covered her, as I had been covered, head and all, in three rugs. She looked an odd figure, like a canary covered for the night. Dawn came, the cold was as intense as ever, and the roads were icy. I kept on feeling Mat. Her stillness made me nervous. My mind ran on all the stories I had read, of the torpor that sets in before death from exposure. Over my two coats, I wore a garment called " Great Uncle Tom's Dressing Gown "— thick, heavy, blanket-like, reaching below ankle level, so wide that it folded around me and became double-breasted, so long that the cuffs were twice turned back, and as I walked in it, I gathered up the front to save being tripped. It had once belonged to Kath's Uncle Tom, and had gained its new name because I had felt he must be such a huge man to fit so large a garment.

Fine snow was silently piling the hedges into strange and fantastic shapes, leaning out into the road like the fangs of some prehistoric animal. The whole world had taken on an extremely cruel and relentless look. Before we ascended the pass, we put on chains, and left Dinas Mawddwy, thinking longingly of breakfast with Kath, of blazing fires and warm feet. Near the top of the pass we stopped, for ahead of us was a big car across the road, its nose almost over the drop into the valley below. After some odd manœuvres, which we could not properly make out at that distance, it came creeping down and we started up again. When we reached the same spot, we slewed round and slipped back. The slow turn continued for a few nerve-racking moments, and I waited in horrid anticipation for the moment when we would pitch off the road and down the slope. Fortunately, it never came. The back wheels considerately knocked up against a small rise in the bank, and there we stopped. For a few minutes we cursed the driver of the big car for his unmannerliness in not warning us, especially as our job in crossing the icy patch to get up was going to be much harder than his, going down. We got out to a blizzard blowing up from the pass so aptly named " Bwlch Oerddrws "—the Pass of the Open Door. I thought of the happening Iolo had told me of, of a local man who had deserted his car in the pass in a snowstorm, and for three weeks no one had been able to find it. With pick and shovel we set about converting the appearance of that bit of white landscape, chipping away at the frozen, rocky earth of the mountainside, and carrying our scores of painfully small shovelfuls to scatter on the twenty yard stretch of frozen stream. I was glad of Great Uncle Tom, though his length got in my way, and I found myself driving the pick through his hemline more often than not.

It was, as always, lovely to arrive at Kath's that day, and to feel some life returning to my numbed and leaden feet. When we had had breakfast, we walked up to Blaen-y-cwm, leaving the car at the longhouse until the chance of getting it through the four fields was more certain. It was lovely too, to arrive at Blaen-y-cwm, and look at the snowy landscape through windows instead of windscreen.

The furniture packages lay in the hall waiting to be assembled. By evening, it was ready. We had easy chairs, warmth and comfort. The blue crockery shone, the fire blazed up the immense chimney, and the corner by the bread oven was piled with dry logs. After fetching milk and walking back up the cold, moonlit fields, we used to peer through the lamplit window before going in, for the pleasure it gave us.

Before the Old Year ended, the snow went. The brilliant, high white shapes thawed, and left the mountains beneath, warm and brown, with masses of old wet, red bracken. The barometer pointer swung slowly away from " More Wind," and settled itself in a more encouraging position. We felt we could at last safely tackle the problem of loose and missing slates, and of all the work we did to that house, I think the repair of its roof, and later, the new door and windows we gave it, were what it appreciated most.

It is a courageous little house, standing and facing squarely the rain that beats upon it, unlike some that huddle in hollows and turn their backs to the weather. But lovely as it is to face south to the Cader range, it has its drawbacks. Doors and windows are to the house what buttonholes are to a mackintosh—a chink in the armour as one faces the enemy. The rain blows in and trickles down inside them, and the distance rain could be hurled under the door gap when winds were at their worst, was astonishing. I was determined to put in new doors and windows as soon as possible.

The hope of calm, settled weather gave an opportunity to see to the roof at any rate, and we set off to borrow Willie's ladder.

It was a wonderfully clear, still wintry morning as we walked down the fields. A robin sang his dry, crackling song from the plum tree. Hoar-frost lay thick on the grass, and our footprints left dark patterns across its purity. The little black bullocks stood in a quiet group near the barn, their breath turning to a halo of vapour in the cold air, and the sun, as it struck across their shaggy backs, changed them from black to a warm brown. The longer grasses by the walls, bent beneath their weight of rime, were patterned in exquisite crystalline shapes. Frozen spray from the stream lay like glass on the nearby rocks. The pools of the track were glazed into thin, splintering ice, and for once the muddy patches were hard underfoot. Near the bridge, a squirrel ran along the wall top, a brilliant splash of red, and magpies flew in ones and twos from the bare oaks on the lower mountain.

" There are two men near my father's house," began Willie, " who do repair their roof very quickly." I listened attentively. " They take a bucketful of thin cement up to the very top, and there they do pour it down, and as it runs down they sweep it up again into every little crack."

In theory, it sounded wonderfully efficient, in practice, I wondered, how did it work out ? Carrying a bucketful of cement, is in itself a Herculean task, let alone getting it to the ridge of a roof. Having tipped it out and lost that amount of weight from one side, my natural reaction would be to fall down the other side. As for the cat-like agility of the sweeper, on what did he stand ? Did he walk along the slope of loose tiles in his bare feet, sweeping, or was the roof covered with ladders, and if so, how did he sweep beneath them ?

" I have never done it," said Willie, with a grin that means he had the same doubts, so I told him of my own fancy, which is, a very small, very cheap helicopter. When it has been perfected, and can hover safely, moving up, down or sideways in minute distances, the problem of ever-recurring repair will be solved—except for the purchase of the helicopter.

" We will share one," said Willie, approvingly.

We carried back the great clumsy ladder, and laid it by the house, while we walked round the walls and weighed up the possibilities. It was an awkward roof to attack, for in front, a wall lay just where one wanted to stand the ladder. Even with this snag overcome, I could not see how to manage the next step of getting from the ladder to the roof, and more important still, how to remain there. At the back, a wide gully ran the length of the house, and to bridge this, several feet of ladder had to be wasted. But there, at least, the roof swept sufficiently low for the ladder to be actually laid on it. It gave an easy beginning. What came next, we left to Providence. The main trouble was the great weight of the ladder. To lower it gently was impossible, for as soon as it leaned an inch or two away from the vertical, it took all our strength to hold it. I was afraid that if we tried to lower it on to the roof, we should find it had arrived not only on the roof, but through it. After some thought, we rested the top of it on the edge of the roof. With the household steps opened out to their full length alongside it, I could, by standing on them, slowly pull up the ladder until it was as high as it would go.

At the end of half an hour it was manœuvred more or less into place. Lashed to the top of it was the worm-eaten ladder from the barn ; roped to that came the household steps, and for the last few feet to the coping I took up a little affair of five rungs, a frail, home-made thing, manufactured from hazel poles, which we carried about to use as a sort of Bailey bridge for crossing flooded streams, or to leave, for use as a stile, by the rickety top wall to the lake track.

Viewed from below, the whole structure looked very haphazard, and after one view from above, I preferred not to look again.

We set to work. Mat mixed cement and brought it out to me. Until I arrived at the ridge, she held on to the bottom ladder. The first trip gave me rather a peculiar sensation, for as the house roof lay at a different slope from those of the back places, it was not possible for the ladders to lie flat up the whole expanse. In addition, the ladders themselves were not regular in thickness or shape, so that scaling them worked rather like the canal lock system. On leaving one ladder, and entering the next section, I waited for the levels to equalize themselves, transferring my weight gently from one to the next, and the upper sections, from pointing skywards, gradually lowered themselves to the roof contours. As I moved to the next rung, they all took up their new

D

positions with a series of bumps like the sound of a gently shunted goods train.

Once at the ridge, I was safe, for I sat astride, and scrabbled slowly along to the far chimney with the cement bucket on one arm, but a few traverses were painful with the weight of cement pushing me more firmly on to the sharp ridge. How much easier it would be, I felt, if I could devise a little saddle with rubber castors, propelled, scooter-wise, by paddling the feet.

The ladder joints developed zig-zags at each elbow, but I reflected that if it did concertina at the joints, collapse would be slow enough for me to slide gracefully down with it, and give me time to choose a landing place on the grass, instead of, as at the front, a vertical drop on to a stone wall.

By the time the barometer had slipped back to " More Wind " again, the chimney leaks and as many loose tiles as I could reach by stretching down were finished. It looked a very small fraction of an immense whole, but it was the most we could accomplish that holiday, for when the wind really blew it felt like the top of the world up there, though the sight of the slipped tiles it brought, used to fill me with anguish.

Easter came and we arrived in the lambing season. " I am glad indeed to see you here," said Richard Jones, with satisfaction. " You will help to frighten the foxes."

" How ? " I enquired with interest.

" The smell of your fires will keep them away," he said. " Already we have lost many lambs."

Nevertheless, they came as far as the maternity field that hungry year, and carried off the weaklings. Because of that, we developed the habit of taking the taxi-horn—our dinner-bell—far up into the little cwm before going to bed, and tooting it loud and long to scare them. It made three echoes, and I used to stand, wondering whether it would bring from the darkness, the decrepit ghost of some old London taxi.

That holiday was a silly season for sheep. We found two with their horns firmly entangled in fence netting, and disentangled them at last by seizing them by their thick neck wool, and pulling them out the way they had got in.

Some of them used to leap gullies too wide for their lambs to follow. Beelzebub behaving thus, spent some hours in the wood, leaving her new lamb on the other side of the stream. The stupid mother ate steadily all afternoon, occasionally muttering a " Baa " with her mouth full, not even bothering to raise her head as the bleats became more heartrending. Obviously, motherhood was a responsibility she should not have undertaken, and at dusk, we determined to bring home to her the heinousness of her callous behaviour. We pursued her with leaps and yells up and down the wood, until even motherhood was preferable, and she returned to her grateful and forgiving child.

In the driving sleet of the cold Spring days, the pathetic little things stand miserably under the shelter of the walls, immobile and unhappy in a cruel world. A newly-born one there tore at our sympathies so much that we fetched it in, dried it, and laid it, surprised, but not displeased, in front of the fire. Before long, its mother came blundering to the door, making such a fuss, that we had, perforce, to put the lamb out again into the streaming rain and wind. This time, it looked definitely displeased, but by Whitsuntide, it had grown fat and sturdy and impervious to weather.

Whitsuntide brought us a new bull—a black and evil devil, compared with whom, our first one was a household pet. With this one I never felt safe unless at least two fields separated us. He glowered and brooded the whole day long, walking restlessly round his limiting walls, lashing his tail, and regularly, when dark fell, he started the most blood-curdling bellows, which smashed in great vibrating waves on the rocks of the Garn.

We lay awake listening to him, and then, gradually, as dark deepened he calmed down, and the fury receded like a thunderstorm dying away as it travels towards some other horizon.

There was only one consoling aspect to his sojourn there, and that was, that because of his savagery, the walls of the field had been built up and reinforced with great tree trunks, but the day he escaped, even this solace was removed, and our faith in the tree trunks was considerably jolted, to say the least.

We walked to the lake one afternoon, and skirting the shores, ambled slowly home. Leaving the mountain proper, we were halfway across a stretch of open moor when we saw that the group of bullocks which Blaen-y-cwm nurtures was grazing in a shadowed angle of the walls. As they moved slowly along, a gap between them suddenly disclosed the bull, standing arrogantly among them like a sixth-form bully among the lower fry. No one needed to explain to anyone else that there was the bull and we must run. Without a word, we ran, and he, with one outraged, appraising look, came too. Fortunately, we had a good start. We, with him some distance behind, took the wall of the little wood in one leap, reminiscent of Dirck and Jorick, and once in there, we instinctively took different routes in the hope that he would have to pause and consider which of us would make the more rewarding pursuit. We arrived on the doorstep together, and burst in and crowded to the back window overlooking the slope over which we had just raced. There he was, just beyond our tumbledown walls, sniffing in the sandpit. When our pulses returned to normal, we decided we must fetch Richard Jones, for the savage now out of his field, was on a public track, and although perhaps three people use it from one year's end to the next, Fate, in its incalculable way, might have decreed that this was to be the day. We had not far to go for the men were in the bottom fields.

" He is *out* ? " said Willie, and the expression he put into the words conveyed the impression that Ghengis Khan was abroad. They came up and went to the stable, emerging from it looking like characters from the French Revolution, with forks, ropes, a long axe and thick stakes.

The bull, meanwhile had gone back over the hill out of sight, and we waited to catch the first glimpse of the returning captive. Only the first glimpse, and then we were going inside. I felt like one waiting to see a lyncher brought down, but at the first sound of those awful, soul-shakings bellows, I abjured the intention and went inside again.

For the rest of the holiday, as we fetched our milk at dusk, we gained a modicum of confidence from the knowledge that when the enemy roared, we at least knew where he lay, but even so, it was an alarming journey back in the half light. Imagination and apprehension conjured up such realistically bull-like shapes from a pile of stones, a scrub oak or a shadow, and our hearts leapt a hundred times at the sudden movement of a sheep in the bracken.

August brought several stretches of still weather, and by then, I had worked out how I could repair the front roof by approaching it from the back. We rigged up the usual gimcrack system, and to the topmost hazel ladder I knotted the climbing rope, in such a fashion that I could slide down the front roof dangling at the end of it. Mat, tied to the ladder, pulled me up or let me down from the ridge, as required. It was not a marked success. To prevent me from sliding, the rope had to be taut, but to be able to lean across and replace the loose tiles, I needed a certain amount of slack. Mat, in her anxiety to keep me on the roof, twice pulled too hard on my lead, precipitating me into a helpless spread-eagled sort of position, face to the slates. After a day of this, and very little to show for it, we evolved the better method of making another small hazel-pole ladder, and lowering it down the front from the coping. On these hot, summer days, the slates seemed to sizzle as a trowelful of cement was dropped on them, and they were burningly hot to bare legs. I used to feel very remote up there. Sounds from ground level filtered out, and I only heard the high-up noises from far away,—the bleating of sheep on Craig-y-Deryn, the mewing call of the buzzards, and the ravens' call as they wheeled in the sky, small black specks in the blue over Lliwedd. A voice from below sounded like a voice from the underworld.

I was glad when the front roof was finished, for a vague nervousness crept with me from slate to slate, and I reflected that for such an occupation, I really deserved danger money. To return to the back slope was a relief.

Crawling over it, I discovered one rather appalling thing—the roof of the dairy was at no point really joined to the

roof of the house, but simply leaned hopefully against it.
With such an advantage, it would be easy for the wind to
enter the crack, and with its strong North hand, lever the
building apart. I dedicated the rest of the cement to filling
up the long slit. The job was unutterably wearisome, so
slow, so monotonous, and of such length. I stuck a long
ridge of cement under the back eaves, much like an elongated
swallow's nest, and when it had set, I laid pieces of slate upon
it and cemented them to the lower roof. I used to look with
utter loathing at the length still to be done as I imperceptibly
covered inch after inch. Sometimes the gap was wide, and
difficult to bridge, and occasional plops of cement fell straight
through into the dairy, a soft splash heralding their arrival
on the tiled floor. I kept count, and gathered them up at
each descent, putting them in the mouseholes in the dairy
wall.

The last day, work went slower and slower, and I counted
eleven plops. Sick to the soul of cement, I climbed down
and went to search for them. I could only find six. I
groped under the cupboards and in the dark corners in vain.

Giving it up, I straightened my back, and looked round to
see what we were to have for tea. Tea was decorated with
the lost plops,—a beautiful apple-pie bore a cement decoration, meringue fashion, and the saucepans along the shelf,
bottom upwards, each carried a larger or smaller motif!

Although much remained to be done, the back was
broken, and I felt I could sleep more happily through winter
storms at home, without dreaming that Blaen-y-cwm slates
were sliding off the roof by the dozen.

That idyllic state of mind persisted until we came again,
and found more broken slates on the grass, and from that
time, we faced reality, and the knowledge that the roof,
unless we could spend a summer in taking it off and relaying
it, would never be finished.

Soon after Christmas, I too, was recalled to London.
I left on a day with deep snow, crisp and sparkling in the
sun, and arrived in London to find grey slush, grey skies,
and a winter endlessly prolonged. The days seemed all
alike, and one never saw the changing of the seasons.

But there was one bright spot : I was sent to a boys' school, and my headmaster asked me whether I could teach any kind of craft. I told him, rather doubtfully, that I had done some woodwork. He asked me, even more doubtfully, could I teach it ? I thought I could, if he didn't expect too much.

By the end of that term, I was teaching woodwork all day to hordes of big and little boys, in a beautifully fitted workshop with ten double benches, windows on every side, a timber yard of rare and precious woods in the store room, and cases of tools and implements so strange to me, that I had to pore over Tyzack's catalogue before I could get an inkling of their purpose. Soon we were turning out coffee tables and fireside stools on the Blaen-y-cwm pattern, almost by mass production.

I learnt a good deal in the years I was there, though I used to wonder, uneasily, how I should justify to an inspector, City and Guilds trained, my particular and very individual way of setting out dovetails.

Fortunately, those who came were kind, and turned a blind eye to irregularities, and several of the boys entered the cabinet-making trade at Shoreditch, where I am happy to think that in them, at least, any unorthodox ideas they may have absorbed from me, are now corrected.

CHAPTER VIII

THE time came when the basic ration ceased, and instead of being able to start off to Blaen-y-cwm when we were ready, we had to start at such time as would bring us to Paddington at a moment when the G.W.R. proposed to run a train to Ruabon.

Instead of being able to stow all we meant to take with us into the car, we now had to study a different technique. For a week beforehand we considered. Having considered, we packed ; having packed, we carried the result to the end of the garden and back, and in the face of this enlightening experience, we unpacked and threw out two thirds. As the week progressed, gradually one third would creep back, as Mat or I inserted, in each other's absence, articles that the other had discarded as unnecessary, and on the evening of departure, we turned everything out again and compromised.

Last minute odds and ends went in my pockets. I travelled in slacks (two pockets), suede jacket (two pockets), and mac. (two pockets). Unfortunately, the pockets overlaid each other on the same place each side, and by the time I was accoutred, my hips were twice their normal size, making the passing of other travellers in train corridors a thing to be avoided.

With bulging rucksacks, and shatteringly loud, hobnailed footsteps we walked down the mile of quiet road to our small Essex station. Arrived there, I was invariably wishing that we had been more ruthless in our rejections, but this wore off, for after we had pushed in and out of carriages, been swept backwards and forwards in the Underground, and wafted along with the crowds entering Paddington, our burdens became a habit, and we staggered along like Christian, in and out of our sloughs of despond.

At this time, the L.N.E.R. seemed to run only its oldest

rolling-stock. It appeared to be a great effort for some of it to roll at all, and the train would clank along, almost at its last gasp, necessitating a stop at every station for a rest. There were fourteen stations. I would have liked to see, in daylight, the engine that hauled us up to Liverpool Street that first winter. I imagine it would bear a strong resemblance to the Rocket.

The carriages, too, were very old, very dirty, very dusty. The dim, artificial lights glimmered on ancient photographs of seaside resorts in a species of dismal blue-grey colour. I suspect that they were so old that the seaside resorts have long ceased to exist, washed away by the encroaching currents of the North Sea.

Paddington had long queues, spreading in serpentine curves from each platform gate back to the Underground entrance. We arrived early, and seeing the queue, hoped that it meant " First come, first served," but it was a vain hope, for just before the train was due in, the gates were opened, and the hordes entered to a fair field and no favour.

We surged forward, and went through the usual wartime weighing up of the best place to stand. Rarely, on any journeys, did the train come to rest leaving a third-class door exactly opposite to us. Oh, the hopes and fears !—the beating hearts of those last few minutes, when luggage has been gripped and teeth gritted, and one waits ! So often a door would seem to be stopping conveniently just by us. I would stretch out an eager hand to grasp the handle, and it would give an indignant jerk and glide further down the platform. Some passengers, with no idea of the rules of the game, like motorists who wait at the traffic signals with bottom gear already engaged and clutch depressed, would grab the handle of the carriage of their choice, and hanging firmly on to it, walk down the platform with it until it stopped, sweeping aside all those poor fools who felt they could only regard a carriage as theirs if it stopped providentially exactly in front of them.

We grew quite fatalistic about this aspect of train travel. It was no good dodging hither and thither ; one just stood stoically, waiting for what Fortune might bring, and Fortune usually brought a first-class coach, the doorless middle of a corridor, or the guard's van.

None of the day trains arrived in time for us to air the house and settle in before dark. The only one that arrived early enough to give us time for this left Paddington five minutes after midnight, and arrived about nine-thirty in the morning. On this we had decided to travel, arguing that most potential travellers would prefer to be in bed at 12.5, and therefore the train would be less crowded ; but the people who should have gone to bed by midnight, plus the people who, like us, had banked on this supposition, had all turned up for the 12.5.

The corridor travellers were just a smooth sheet of flattened garments pressed closely upon the windows, looking like tinned tongue in a glass mould. We joined them, and there we stood the whole night long, propped up by the pressure of other standing bodies, not daring to move our feet for more than a few inches, for Lebensraum surrendered was difficult to regain. The only change of position we could get was obtained by changing places with each other, revolving around a very small point in a great number of intricate movements, like some Oriental dancer, until one or other of us was in the better position of being able to lean against the window, without having lost any of our total area.

The air of Ruabon that morning, seemed very sweet, and to be able to move one's limbs again was ecstasy. We drank our coffee outside the dismal waiting room, for there was neither waiting room fire, nor open refreshment room. At Corwen, the refreshment room was open and inviting, but the train only stopped for a few seconds ; long enough to give one a tantalizing glimpse of a warm-looking interior, with sandwiches and steaming cups of tea and coffee being handed over a shining counter to leisurely looking people, before they slid from our hungry eyes.

I loved the journey beyond Bala. It had, not stations, but Halts, small wooden huts and tiny platforms like part of a toy-train set. They stood in the vast expanse of moor with, perhaps, one country woman in black, waiting with basket and rolled umbrella. The Halts had a sort of romantic aura for me, and that aura was increased one snowy winter evening when we passed through on the last train. Single wick oil lamps were burning dimly above the platforms of the Halts. We stopped at them all, the guard got out and walked to the lamps through the thick, whirling snow, and carefully turning them out, garnered them into his van. The Halts had done their duty for the day. We pulled out and left them in darkness and snow, in the midst of the silent moor and white mountains.

On this morning we wandered on beyond Bala, waiting once for the up train to come in before we could venture out on the single line. I watched for the place in the pass where the stream changes its direction of flow as we cross the water-shed, and after the laborious, breathless climb up the gradient, the engine gave a joyful shriek, gathered speed and careered happily down to Bont Newydd. I enjoyed the unhurried movements of the local passengers alighting at the stations. Watching them, I would still hear the raucous shouts of last night at Liverpool Street Underground :

" Hurry along there, please ! Mind the doors ! " The lack of fevered scurry, the leisureliness, the minutes the driver could afford to wait for a late passenger, the way the guard popped his head into the carriage and chatted to us, and popped out again to give a friendly salute towards the signal-box, had a strong appeal to me. It was always the right beginning for the timeless days at Blaen-y-cwm.

But getting there was only one aspect of life at Blaen-y-cwm. There was also the smaller scale problem of moving other things, beside ourselves, up and down the valley. Since our last holiday, Enid had married and moved down the valley, so that we now had a twice weekly bread problem. There were also, as well as general shopping, the heavier things at longer intervals to be coped with ; though once, when we were down to our last few lumps of coal, Evan Jones, crashing through all precedents, ventured over our bridge with his tractor, and brought us a load of coal to the very door, a small version of the Relief of Lucknow.

Willie had sold his horse, and bought instead a small second-hand van of uncertain habits. The change was not necessarily progress. When the van ran, we had its assistance, for it could reach Blaen-y-cwm before the last drop of water leaked from its radiator. Through the long periods when it did not even run, but stood obstinate and immobile on the grass outside Willie's house, we had to fend for ourselves.

The cart I had made had been in Wales for some time. Kath and a friend walked to the station with it when our train was due, and drew it up on the platform as impressively as though she had brought shooting brake and ghillie from the Lodge.

We packed the rucksacks in, and emptied the contents o my six pockets. We collected our previously ordered bottles of beer from " The George," and tucked them into the corners. I put in my mac., Mat added her coat, and the *cortège* proceeded across the bridge. The toll-bridge keeper smiled as usual, and as usual hoped the long, long trail would not be too long. The station master was amused, but for me the event had all the excitement of launching a ship. The cart rolled along, silently and easily.

At the bottom of the hill, Iolo was waiting with our groceries, and with two on the handle and Iolo on the trace rope, they climbed the hill, Mat and I walking lazily and gratefully behind.

By the chapel, we left it while we went up to Kath's for breakfast, and the team turned out again to help us up the second steep slope. Reaching the top, we all sat down on the bank, and smoked while we rested. Then the helpers departed, leaving us of the upper cwm to proceed alone with our little cart.

It travelled well so long as the surface was good, but to pull it over the raised rocks in the road was difficult, and as the road became worse, tugging became strenuous. Up the wet and stony stream-bed, our progress became slower, and the pulling hard indeed. In summer the stream-bed track never dries, in winter a torrent pours over it, and in really bad weather, half the bog and the whole of the bridge are submerged beneath the flood. The end of the long journey when we dragged it through the humped field with the wet earth sucking at its tyres reduced us to near despair and deep desperate silence, in which I tried to forget the discomforts in much the same way as I face the dentist, with the thought, " In ten minutes this will all be over." And in all the journeys we were forced to make in this manner, the agony never lessened.

However, the cart, unlike the sled, was a success from the beginning, and carried far more than the hundredweight recommended by the smith who made its axle. Loaded with logs, its tyres were often as flat as though they were punctured.

At the end of every holiday, we trundled our rucksacks and laundry to Kath's, and leaving the cart in her barn, ready for the next holiday, walked to the station with our packs.

We used it to return Iolo's step ladder which we had borrowed again. Lashing it to the cart early one morning, we started off down the fields. On the level area through the birches, I persuaded Mat, with some difficulty, to sit on the top. I felt that only by riding on it could she appreciate how easily it ran. We cantered along in the sunshine, Mat perched high on the horizontal step-ladder, and clinging, without much appearance of enjoyment, to its sides. Turning a bend in the track, we met an astonished-looking elderly couple, and flashed past, leaving them staring after us. It was rarely that we met walkers, and we were rather surprised to see any so early. They were obviously far more surprised at what they saw—a small cart coming down from the mountains bearing a step-ladder surmounted by a rather apprehensive-looking figure, pushed by another figure in distemper splashed overalls. We were out of sight quickly enough for them to be able to feel that we were an hallucination.

After we had given the cart a long trial, we felt that we needed something quicker as well, and supplemented it with a bicycle for ordinary shopping expeditions. On a bicycle, we could ride part of the way down to the bottom, and all the way to Dolgelley and back, and pushing it up the hills, we could hang the bags on the handlebars. It was no harder than walking, and much quicker in total time, for we were independent of bus or train, and even coming back, there were rideable stretches.

But it was the wrong type of bicycle, for the only one we could find in time for our next sojourn had a back pedal brake. Except for one with a fixed wheel, it was the most unsuitable machine we could have for our kind of country. Had it owned an ordinary free wheel, it would have been possible to keep one pedal or the other from knocking against upstanding rocks on the route. With a back-pedal brake we were helpless. More than helpless, for if the pedals could not be worked round out of the way of a snag in time, the bicycle slewed fiercely as a pedal caught, and off the rider came. In a few days both pedals were bent backwards, and one rode, unavoidably, in Chaplinesque manner, with heels in and toes out, almost at right-angles.

The animals added to our difficulties. They always lay, very naturally, but to my great irritation, in the smoother dryer parts of the way. Going down in a hurry one day, I saw ahead of me, six bullocks sprawled across the track, sunning themselves. To avoid them meant riding into the soft bog. They had to be urged up quickly. " Get up ! Get up ! " I shouted. " Can't you see I'm in difficulties ? " and made a noise sounding as near to the voice of the hearthrug dog as I could manage. They lumbered slowly to their feet, chewing their cud, and whisking their tails, and disclosed, sitting on a rock beyond, two sheepish-looking hikers also rising to their feet. I, too, felt rather sheepish, as I explained that I was talking, not to them, but to the bullocks.

Sometimes, when she was tired of the back-pedal brake and its dangers, Mat walked down and caught the bus, and I cycled to the bottom to meet her on her return. We hung all the packages on the bicycle and took turns to push. Then we evolved a quicker method that worked well for weeks. We halved the packages, and took turns cycling along, and the rider would get off when it suited her, leave the bicycle propped against the tree or wall, and walk on. The walker came along, picked up the machine and overtook the walker ahead, leaving the transport again when she grew tired of it. So it went on until we reached home. We had no definite places for leaving it, and one day I dropped it hurriedly in a bed of bracken because I could see a heron on the bank of the stream with his back to me. I crept up and watched until he sensed me and flew off, and forgetting I had the bicycle I walked on. I waited to be overtaken, but the usual interval went by without Mat making an appearance. I reached home, and there was still no sign of her. After a considerable time she arrived on foot, sagging with parcels.

" Where's the bicycle ? " I asked, surprised. " I couldn't find it," said she, somewhat bitterly. After that we had recognized stops for it, and I traipsed down in order to retrieve a bicycle with its parcels, when I had planned to spend a long August afternoon on the Garn.

The rough, unsheltered life the bicycle led increased its liability to minor ailments, and the day the right-hand pedal broke off entirely we had, perforce, to resort to our old practice of shopping on foot until we could get a new spindle. We staggered over the mountain, bowed down with pickle, jam and marmalade jars, as well as limejuice bottles, wondering whether it had occurred to manufacturers in their cut-throat competition, that, other things being equal, the maker who tins, rather than bottles, could sweep the board of his rivals. It is not only the weight of the bottles, but the way they bang together and break. A broken jar of beetroot can create a frightful mess when it reaches the flour and sugar.

Passing Cwm Mynach Isaf with the shopping, always brought out the dogs. Often we tried to bribe them with tremblingly offered biscuits, but, like the Danegeld, it was bad policy. It proved only a sort of delaying tactics, which started furious fights, and made them not the smallest amount more kindly disposed towards us. Indeed it was worse ; they pursued us savagely for more. One happy day we discovered the best defence. The best defence was offence, but when we came upon it we did not immediately recognize it as such. I had bent to tie my shoelace, Mat guarding my rear, when there was a sudden hush, and they all dashed away into the bracken. It was wonderful, like being able to conjure up a protecting genii. I looked round to see whence came our salvation, but there was no one in sight. The dogs, cowering in the undergrowth, let us go in peace, and it was not until we were half-way home that it came to us—they thought we were going to stone them, and had taken my bending figure as the preliminary to picking up a handful. Fetching milk lost its terrors—a swift bend from the waist was enough to scatter the pack. For long I wished that I could instruct foxes in the art of stone-throwing.

It was at about this time that we tried to make a garden. Looking out from the kitchen window one morning, Mat noticed that the old holly seemed to be looking rather sere and yellow. Its leaves were dropping and the top half of the tree was mere skeleton—dry and lifeless. Besides being an æsthetic disaster, it was a misfortune in more utilitarian ways, for to its westerly branch was secured an end of the clothes-line, and the northerly one helped to support our only drainpipe.

Next time Richard Jones came up we asked him what he thought of it ; was it merely sick and amenable to treatment, or was it dead and beyond hope ?

" It will die," he said, pointing to the lack of bark at the base. " The sheep came down from the mountain in the winter when we had much snow. There was no grass, and hunger drove them to eat the bark of the trees."

When we suggested growing a new one he was rather discouraging, and quoted a Welsh proverb : " If you want a holly by your house, you must build your house by a holly."

Pondering on this, I wondered why ; were they slow or merely sulky ?

" I do not know," he said. " But it is so."

We felt it was worth trying to see whether the proverb erred. Such presumption, I suppose, deserved retribution, but there were plenty of hollies about, and by transferring one quickly we thought it might be induced to take root again before it noticed its change of position.

At first our ambitions were quite modest ; a bush reaching as high as the wall tops would satisfy us, and holly-hunting became a reason for starting off in new, unexplored directions. When we had had enough of indoor toil and moil for the day, we started off on outdoor toil and moil as a change.

There was a magnificent berried one in the wood, standing

SAWING LOGS

THE HALL WITH NEW FRONT DOOR AND FANLIGHT, HALL SEAT
AND THREE-LEGGED TABLE

so high among the oaks that we could see it from the dairy window. In winter it made a welcome green splash among the leafless branches around it, and reminded me that " of all the trees that are in the wood the holly bears the crown." But it had brought up no offspring ; not the merest seedling grew on the earth beneath.

The little cwm had several small ones, but, like the oaks struggling up through the piles of stones collected by some forgotten husbandman, they had been eaten into such curious shapes that they looked as though never again could they be induced into holly shape after such an unfortunate beginning.

In the sinister-looking Gamlyn valley beyond Craig-y-Deryn, a length of tussocky, dangerous bog, with six deserted houses and a river that floods out wide at the slightest provocation, we found several—shapely and not too big.

The lake cwm had rather a nice one, but when we discovered it we had neither pick nor shovel with us. When we returned, although we searched all morning, it had gone, or at least it was not to be found. I think it is quite possible that trees in the lake cwm walk about, at any rate when night falls.

We noted down all we had found, and reduced them to a short list of three. After giving each a final interview, we decided on one in the Gamlyn valley, and late one afternoon set out to fetch it home. It was about three feet tall, and shapely, but whether it would bear berries we had no means of knowing. We had to gamble on that, for at such a tender age there was no indication as to what it would be when house-high.

Dusk was falling as we got it into its carefully prepared hole. We soused the ground around it and went in to supper. After a few minutes we heard a sound with which we had become very familiar—the dry, rattling sound of shaken holly branches. The sheep were nibbling its leaves. So were the lambs, the meek and gentle lambs. In a few days its leaves, except for those at the very top out of reach, were eaten.

The mentality of the so-called domesticated animals of

that valley is beyond my understanding. Everything was native, and they could have had it at any time by just wandering around their usual beats. But no !—that was not enough. Like someone else's toy, ours was nicer. Had we planted a berberis hedge and tried to make clematis grow up the walls, I could have understood them, and perhaps forgiven them for wanting a new taste on their bored palates, but what *could* one think, except that, like the little boy in *Alice in Wonderland*, they only did it to annoy because they know it teases?

Very early in this period of hope we had considered buying twenty red-barked willows to plant along the stream to look warm and glowing against the grey walls in winter, but in a very short time we knew, quite finally, that no consideration was needed.

After a brief experience of the Blaen-y-cwm animals, I ceased to believe the theory that plants are given prickly leaves to protect them against those who would eat them. As we morosely watched the decrepit old ewes chewing them it was plain we must find a taller tree beyond their reach, and that, moreover, we must protect its trunk by wrapping layers of wire netting around it.

The next holly was much larger. It leaned out horizontally over a deep pool, with its roots growing in soft, squelchy mud. It looked easy. We dressed for the part and went up to wrestle with it.

There is a delightful book by Kapek called *The Gardener's Year*. One of its drawings gives a kind of wiring diagram of root systems. From experience of that bog holly I can testify to its truth. It tends, if anything, to understatement. Old gardening lore has it that a tree's roots extend as far as its branches, but the roots of the bog holly did more. After extending branch length they dived branch deep. At the end of two hours we had an elaborate series of channels running in a wide radius from the trunk, like the scale model of a delta. The channels, as we dug, filled quickly with water, and along the bottom of each was a root dipping down for an unknown distance.

Next day we managed to lift them and bore the holly

over the quarter mile of mountain separating it from its new site. Mat carried its roots while I took its head, firmly bound up in ropes, and here I should like to debunk another theory on hollies—that they are only prickly at the bottom to dis-courage animals, thus making for the survival of the species. This holly was fifteen feet high, and as prickly one end as the other. If the theory *is* correct, the only conclusion is that long-necked pachyderms still live and graze up there, and although I can almost believe this, I do not wish to.

Next morning, as I sat up in bed, I could just see the top of it gently waving outside the window. We were extremely pleased with it. As we walked up the fields its dark green stood out against the grey house-front. I visualized it in old age ; its own and ours; of immense girth, its heavy branches dotted thickly with brilliant scarlet berries. But, alas ! it never saw old age. After living, apparently con-tented, through a winter and a spring, it chose to die at the end of summer. Its leaves grew brown and shrivelled and dropped off, and although we said that even an evergreen must lose its leaves some time, the brown crackly carpet grew thicker beneath it, and no green leaves came to replace them.

It was nice to have had it, and I cannot think why it clung on so long before choosing to give up. Still, it lived and gladdened us for a time. "What cause of plaint have I, who perish in July ? I might have had to die, perchance in June."

When we came in winter no green bush stood out against the grey walls. Instead was a thin grey trunk, with dry and rattling branches shivering in the wind. We bowed to the wisdom of the Welsh proverb, and in the early spring we fetched a little birch from the wood. It, too, looked lovely for a season, and then some horned beast broke through the wire netting and ate off its bark.

Iolo suggested we had planted the wrong kind of tree. " What you should have put in for those animals," he said, " is a tree of the Knowledge of Good and Evil, and if ever I see one I'll get a cutting for you."

Honeysuckle came next—so entwined about a young rowan tree that when it was unwound it leapt back like a gramophone spring as soon as I relaxed my hold, and I had to carry it home coiled round me, like a snake around its charmer. It suffered the same fate as the birch.

Looking idly through a nurseryman's catalogue some time later, a note on tree planting caught my eye. " Planting of trees over four or five feet high should be left to experts." Since I cannot but feel that no expert would accept an invitation to come and plant a twenty-foot holly at Blaen-y-cwm, we gave up trees. But those experts who plant fifty-foot elms, do they ever, I wonder, when the tumult and the shouting have died, turn up one morning and find them dead ? I suppose that even if they do they hush it up and we hear no more of it. Experts get reputations on success.

When we were thinning out a row of old hawthorns at home we came across one of manageable dimensions and were tempted to try it out, just to see what the animals made of its long, tough thorns. In the end it never got there, mainly because I feared we might transport more than thorns. The largest of the hawthorns stands outside my window. It is the headquarters of the British Sparrows' Association, which meets at three-thirty every Sunday morning through summer. When the quorum is met, Bedlam could not be more distracting. It seemed a tempting of Fate to take a hawthorn tree to Blaen-y-cwm. Sparrows have never lived there, and I am not particularly anxious that they should. The hawthorn was very small, but so are sparrows ; moreover, they are persistent and wily creatures. It was quite feasible that they would, somehow or other, smuggle a lot of other little sparrows into the tree, and as we took it off in the darkness we should take them with us and arrive next day to find that we had been instrumental in founding a branch of the Welsh Sparrows' Association.

The hankering for a garden burgeoned again, though not so ambitiously. No trees figured in the scheme. At Bettws-y-Coed we had seen the bouldered stony slopes surrounding an old cottage planted with gorse and heather, thyme, foxglove and fern. I could imagine the green enclosure within our tumbled walls in a like glory. We confined ours to the front of the house, where we could more easily keep an eye on it.   The stream could be the foundation of a bog garden, gay with yellow iris and bog bean, and the slope was to run up in a riot of purple heather, creeping, sweet-smelling thyme, bog asphodel, sundew and butterwort.

We started first on the nettles, whose heads we had scythed off early in our tenancy—a mistaken policy, which had brought results resembling those of Hercules with the many-headed Hydra.   Now we went to the root of them, digging up the long yellow tangles with a farmyard fork, tracing them doggedly for yards beneath the grass, uphill and down, through bracken and under walls, until we had exterminated every bit we could find.   It was effective.   They have never reared their ugly heads since.

We modified our first ideas and decided to have our garden on the walls, in the hope that the sheep would not notice it. We tipped buckets and buckets of earth on top of the boulders. While searching for plants we found a lush green patch in the field, with orchis of an extraordinarily deep purple, and harebells and violets of unusual size.   The green patch spread, and we found other still bigger and better specimens on it.   Only when the green patch began to rise and hump itself above the surrounding turf did we think of asking why it behaved so.   " Ah, yes—that," said Willie.   " It is my father's old horse.   He died soon after you went back, and we buried him in the bog.   It was a handy place."

The hump rose higher and higher, and we gave it a wide berth in case it exploded.   Gradually it subsided, and after a year or so the vegetation returned to normal.

I made a gate and fence to keep out the cattle, for they had developed a sense of knowing when they could safely come in ;   they knew when we were in bed, and they used to watch us with pleasure whenever we went shopping.   At those times they had a nasty habit of coming in and chewing the washing hanging on the line.   Or they would rub their itchy heads on our knocker early in the morning and startle us with loud knocks at untowards moments.   They would fight each other between the narrow confines of the house and the low wall in front of it, their horns knocking off the coping stones with a resounding crash as they swung round to the escape or the attack. In order to scratch their backs they put their necks under the bars of my fence, and eventually uprooted it. I opened the door one morning early, and the alarmed scratcher, wedged well underneath the fence, jumped and galloped off, bearing with him, around his neck, gate and fence like some enormous yoke. The rams were a nuisance, too, butting at their shining reflections in the chromium hub caps of the car, and the bullocks developed a curious taste for cellulose paint—one lick of their rough, sandpaper tongues and the gloss is gone for ever. They have odd fancies, and will fight for the possession of a bit of chewed rope, and stand for long periods crunching coal—ignoring the cabbage stalks and other greenery we throw to them. Perhaps they are still cutting their teeth, and it is simply juvenile exuberance.

When the fence was in again we developed terrorist tactics and guerilla warfare. As soon as they came near the house we dashed out and chased them off. To make them feel nervous we hid behind walls, and suddenly leapt up to startle them. We kept handy, on the hall table, the old taxi horn. Along with this was a whistle and a heavy bell on a leather strap. When the animals overstepped the bounds we allowed them, Mat would seize whistle and bell, while I snatched the horn, and with these noises we pursued them until energy gave out. Like Pavlov in his experiments, we conditioned them, but with opposite results ; when they heard the bell they galloped not to their food, but from it.

We regretted the necessity, for they were friendly little beasts ; but any inhibitions we managed to put into them they forgot when we met them off the immediate home ground. As we knelt, poking out the thin, thready roots of thyme, they would amble up to us in a little inquisitive group, dribbling and breathing down our necks as they craned over our shoulders to see what we were up to.

The terrifying tactics had to begin again each holiday. They forgot all they had learnt, and there were always new-comers, with whom we had to begin again the first steps in a calf's education.

The walls, so long as we were there to protect them, looked

dazzling in brilliant colourful patches of blue, yellow, purple and green against a background of grey. It was a short-lived pleasure and always ended with the holiday. By spring, when everything should have been sprouting up strong and green, all was nibbled down brown and short, and the sheep had taken the walls into their regular grazing ground. It was not so much that one could not tame the mountain, but that one could not tame the inhabitants.

There is only one thing we can plant and leave, knowing that it will still be there and flourishing when we return, and that is—mint. I suspect that sheep know that, in the Elysian fields they will enter after death, there will be such a superfluity of mint that in life they can well afford to leave it alone.

That year of the garden we had no bull, but we had a near enough imitation, and that was a bullock with a split personality. In his youth he had promised well as a future bull, but as he grew it became apparent to his owners that he lacked the qualities to make him a worthy father to the future little bulls and heifers of Blaen-y-cwm. He was castrated late, and as a consequence suffered from never being able to make up his mind what he was. Some days he was mild, contemplative and inoffensive ; at other times his wrongs seemed to well up in him ; he became morose, alert and fierce, and it was advisable to give him a wide berth. This was difficult, for being officially a bullock it had occurred to no one that he should be under constraint, and he wandered anywhere, his favourite ground being the track by the bridge. Here, whatever phase he was in, we always selected a few heavy stones before making the traverse. If he approached tossing his head and occasionally goring his horns into the earth as he came, he was a bull, and we stood our ground until it was impossible to miss, and then we threw. A menacing look from him was the signal for the second volley. As a rule that stayed him, and the most he did was to follow us, bellowing and shaking his head.

But the morning we went home the method failed. There he was, standing by the track and staring moodily at his front hooves. He shook his head as we came up with him, and then an idea seemed to come into it, for he turned and walked with us a yard or two behind. Neither the first nor the second volley had any effect, and losing our nerve, we gave it up and walked quickly on. So did he—the trio proceeded along an unpleasantly long stretch to the next gate, the quadruped determined and confident, the bipeds neither.

He seemed to be annoyed about something and snorted occasionally behind us. Suddenly he bellowed and stopped, and I saw out of the corner of my eye that he was tossing sods into the air.

" Shall we run for it ? " muttered Mat.

" At the bend," I murmured. " We couldn't beat him to the gate from here."

We took desperately long strides, trying to move more quickly without appearing to hurry, and at the bend we made a dash. A few yards from the gate we heard his galloping hooves on the hard road. Fumbling at the gate and taking twice as long as usual in our panic, we just managed to get through and shut it before he came.

Almost on his heels came dogs. Willie had seen him and sent aid, and for once the dogs were ranged on our side. It was fortunate for us that this animal could accept an accomplished fact. We were safe—until next time—and his enemies were upon him. He stood looking balefully after us; but had he known it only a length of rotten string kept the gate shut.

CHAPTER IX

BACK in Essex, I began on the new front door, a solid thing of two-inch elm planks. This was the peak of my constructional period, as far as size goes. The door was tremendously heavy, for I made new door jambs three inches square and ten feet high, with a three-paned fanlight above and a heavy oak door sill below. The mortises in the door frame were five inches deep, and half-way through the first —almost an evening's work—I peered into it as into a tunnel, and wondered whether I should ever emerge at the other end.

On the day when I fitted its great steel-washered brass hinges, its Yale lock, handle and the three sheets of glass forming the fanlight, I considered holding a celebration. It would have been premature, for the thing still had to be packed, transported and fitted.

We got it off a fortnight or so before we left. Our own journey was bad, for we had tried a method used twice before with great success—to go down the subway on Platform One in the few moments it was left unguarded, to emerge on Platform Three as the only inhabitants. We were not in the train, it is true, but we could take up a stance on the platform instead of being in the back layer of the disinherited —of those with no hope of a seat. After this third trial we never attempted it again, not because of any intrinsic fault in the method, but because our experiences at the third attempt effectively conditioned us against it for ever. We became allergic to subways. For on that August Bank holiday the G.W.R., forsaking long-established tradition, ran the twelve-five from another platform. We had arrived on Number Three, a vast empty space, and were standing happily there, happy because for once no one else seemed to want to go to Reading, Oxford, Banbury, Leamington, Birmingham, Wolverhampton, Wellington, Shrewsbury or Ruabon, despite the fact that there were only fifteen minutes to departure time. I felt deeply grateful to all those towns issuing little booklets describing their holiday attractions, thus draining off all the usual holiday makers from the twelve-five. I blessed the tendency of so many of my countrymen on bank holidays—to rush to the very edge of Britain and to turn their backs on it and gaze longingly away—out to sea.

But when at eleven-fifty the train was still not in we began to feel vaguely disturbed. It seemed to be a very wholesale rush to the edge. At eleven fifty-five we were very definitely disturbed. Surely trains were run as announced, if only for two passengers ? I left my pack with Mat, stole quickly back up the subway, and searched out the indicator board. The twelve-five was not leaving from Platform Three at all ; it was already at Platform Five, and I saw in a horror-struck glance that the battle was already over ; the victors were seated and the vanquished standing. I fled back down the subway, skidding round the corners in my hobs, and up the slope to Mat.

" Quick ! " I gasped. " Platform Five ! It's going in a minute ! "

Down the subway we rushed, and up to Platform Five. Oh ! horrible sight ! Not a passenger on the platform, and at every window discouraging looks and obstructionist attitudes.

I made for a door, and from the dark a voice said, " No room in here. Try next door." But we were getting in that train if it meant fighting him to do it. We wrenched open the door, Mat gave a push, and there was a quick scuffle as standing people staggered closer still and those seated pulled back their feet quickly to avoid having them trodden on. To receive one person with a rucksack in an already crowded compartment is bad enough. To receive two is almost impossible. For a second or two Mat's fate hung in the balance. Half in, half out, she stood on the step clinging to the door, while I tried to get her jammed rucksack frame clear and pull her in. Then the guard came along, turned her quickly sideways, gave her a push and slammed the door. We were in !

On the way up the valley next morning we saw Enid, now settled in a farm lower down the valley. She said she

would come down with us later in the week to collect the
door and a couple of bomb-damaged window-frames we had
bought for a pound. These I had reglazed and repainted,
and the lot awaited us at the station.

We called for Enid on our third evening. She had just
finished churning, and when at length the pale yellow slabs
of butter, each with an imprint of bog myrtle, were laid
upon the purple slate slabs of her dairy, we went out to
catch Polly. Polly was sulky and temperamental at first,
but a trip to the station evidently appealed to her. She
cheered up after a mile, and we bumped down the valley
on the iron-tyred trap wheels at a good pace. There were
no brakes, so down the hill Mat and I helped to keep its
speed in check by hanging on to the back.

Although the packages filled the trap, we bumped our
way back almost as quickly as we had descended, for Polly
was a female Samson, and when at one brief resting-place
I was left to hold Polly, her strength alarmed me. She
tossed her head haughtily, and I was almost lifted into the
air. No wonder a horse seemed to find a sled such child's
play. By the end of the evening I felt that the rating of cars
by horsepower was entirely misleading. So much depends
on the horse. With a Polly two-horse-power car, one could
have climbed Ben Nevis.

We banged and jolted along the Canol track, and every
jolt made her quicker and angrier. We exerted all our
strength behind to try to stem her progress, but were dragged
relentlessly on, over ruts and boulders, with no slackening of
speed. Across the rickety bridge she took us recklessly near
the edge. Finally, just to show us what she *could* do, she
took the sweeping turn into the last field almost at a canter.
This turn had been one of our pleasures, when we had had
petrol, and were bringing friends from the station for their
first visit. We'd race up the humped field and appear
about to crash through the wall to the wood below, and
then make the sudden swinging turn, disclosing the opening,
just shooting through without scraping—so far. I liked seeing
the quick looks of apprehension it produced—looks immediately wiped off and replaced by those of stern resolve to take

whatever was coming as the front-seat passenger leaned forward and grasped the grab rail. Childish, but exhilarating !

Polly's passage was less fortunate. There was a horrible crash and lurch, and as we clung to the back stays of the trap I gave a hurried look round, and saw the gate post lying flat with a foot or two of collapsed wall beside it. At the gate to the lane, frailest of all, the perverse creature stopped, although, judging from her earlier exploits, she could have swept through without even being conscious that it was shut. We felt she would be better out of the shafts while we unloaded. I could see her, ruthless and obliging, taking the burden straight into the house, razing down the walls as she went. Released from harness, she wandered off meekly, tearing up genteel little mouthfuls of grass with the air of a pensioned-off pit pony.

We struggled to get the things off the trap, slid them along the grass into the hall and had a meal. Enid's reaction to the trip was heartening. She hadn't enjoyed an evening so much for a long time, so she told us. Even when Polly trotted up the mountain, refusing to be caught until at last she made a wrong move and we got her into a corner, her spirits were bubbling. She had that happy sort of disposition that gets pleasure from simple things and becomes hilarious over difficulties. I remember one dark and drizzly morning when half a dozen obstinate little black bullocks suddenly cavorted out of the mist on to the track before us. A few minutes later a panting and beaming Enid appeared.

" We're having such fun," she said. " They don't want to go to the station." And back home they all galloped again, Enid following breathlessly behind.

Fitting the door took all next day. By the evening the news that we had a new door had spread, and we were showing it off by lamplight.

Richard Jones prodded it with his stick in the way he prods his bullocks, and gave it his highest praise.

" It is a very strong door," he said. Strength is a primary virtue to the mountain dweller. As he left, it shut with a heavy bang, sounding very final, very locked-up for the night.

Snags arose over fitting the windows. We had thought that the two front windows were the same size, but we found that the opening in the Gladstone-Disraeli room was two inches narrower than that of the kitchen. Chipping away the plaster to try to make it fit was no use, for when we were down to the stonework it was still too narrow.

Next day we removed the two panes of glass, and with an entirely inadequate kit of tools set about cutting down the window-frame. My technique fell a long way that day. I had recourse to plastic wood again. Even worse was the business of cutting down the glass. I understand that glass-cutting needs confidence, and circumstances were such that I had none. I knew that if it went wrong we must go to Dolgelley and carry up two new panes, and the thought was no help to what little confidence I had. But the step had to be taken. I poised the wheel of the cutter above the pane, and with a nervous hand scratched the fateful cut along the makeshift ruler. It made a ragged little line, producing a lot of tiny glass splinters, and then Mat held the glass firmly while I tried to raise enough courage to break it. When I pressed, it bent, but refused to break, and I found this took away from the small amount of confidence I had. We covered it with newspaper so as not to see it bending, and tried again. There was a sharp crack and I had a separate piece in my hand, which I feared would not be the shape we wanted. Nor was it. I fearfully lifted the newspaper and found the cut had a long, sweeping curve to it, and a large part of one corner had broken away. Depressed, I started on the second piece. Now that we had to go to Dolgelley anyhow, I had more confidence. It didn't matter much if I broke this one too, as I did, although not quite so badly.

Getting the new panes was a frustrating experience. First we were told that we needed a licence, and when we found a shop that didn't know about licences, they had no one with confidence, and we had to wait all morning until the cutter came back from a job. Then we had to get it into a crowded train without breaking it or being seen by officials, for I felt sure that large sheets of glass were prohibited articles

in their long and forbidding list. We guarded it in the
corridor, flanked by a large woman who talked angrily and
volubly in Welsh to anyone who cared to listen. I tried to
behave as though I were deaf, cupping my ear when Mat
spoke to me, for the words " Guard's Van " and " Glass "
in English came round regularly.

When the windows were finished and painted, upstairs
as well as down, we took a stroll down the fields to judge the
appearance, and were ridiculously pleased with it. Cream
paint, in place of the dark and weatherworn green, gave the
house an air of having suddenly opened its eyes and wakened
after long hibernation. It looked out with an alive expression and found what it saw was to its liking.

Trudging up the humped fields one day with the week's
shopping, a new shopping solution suddenly came to us—
to buy an old motor-cycle. Age did not matter so long as
it could take the hills, both up and down, negotiate the
rutted track, and fight its way up the stream bed. As I
found when we got it, the rider does most of the fighting ;
the cycle merely carries.

The idea of having a motor-cycle again rather appealed
to me. A wave of nostalgia swept over me as I thought of
my earlier experiences with the internal combustion engine.
We had in Cheshire an engineer friend, a sort of magician
with anything mechanical. If a thing was meant to go,
Percy could make it. He had stayed with us one week-end
and experienced our environment on what Willie graphically
describes as a " shabby day," of heavy rain and savage wind.

We wrote, therefore, to Percy, and asked him to find us a
motor-cycle to stand up to the wear and tear we should
unavoidably put upon it, and asked for one with a magneto,
so that we could leave it, between holidays, without worrying
as to whether its battery was running down in our absence.

Weeks later we arranged to fetch it, travelling to Chester
by train and bringing it back with us in the guard's van,
taking with us Wellingtons, a quart of petrol and oil mixture
from the small ration we were allowed in a ginger-beer
bottle, and an air-cushion which we hoped would serve as
a pillion so that we could both ride up from the station.

The night before we went we stayed with Kath so as to be sure of catching the early train. As Evan Jones passed the longhouse to look at his crops, Kath asked him for the correct time, for after a few days no one is ever quite sure of it. Iolo's clock is only accurate when laid on its face, and for two days it had stood upright. Standing upright, it ticks away, and while wearing a bland and specious look, it contrives to take occasional surreptitious rests at moments when it is likely they will pass unnoticed.

" Indeed, they must not miss the train," said Evan Jones, and gave Kath the time ten minutes fast, omitting to mention the fact lest it destroyed his good intentions. Kath, with the same laudable idea, added ten more minutes. To this combined benevolence I added more so as to have a safety margin, forgetting about it when I strapped on my watch next morning. Finally, Iolo, with a reputation for taking the train before the one he sets out to catch, hurried us off as soon as we had bolted our breakfast. All this well-meant solicitude brought us to the station a full fifty minutes before the train could even be seen crossing the Barmouth bridge. The station was closed and the tollbridge gates were locked. We climbed the fence on to the marshes, hid the petrol bottle in the long grass of the deep ditches running to the river, and wandered about, keeping a wary eye to seaward for the distant puff of smoke along the shore. A flight of ducks flew over the water, looking like a Peter Scott picture, and the cruel-looking swans sailed majestically by on the current. Pink sea thrift was still blooming on the grey-green salt marshes, and sand pipers were whistling somewhere beyond the bend in the bank. We walked along the stream tumbling from our valley to the estuary, and when we saw the station master we turned and strolled back with him. The tiny cotton-wool puffs of engine smoke appeared against the dark woods fringing the estuary. The tollbridge keeper unlocked his gate and hung up his rack of tickets, surprised to see us so early.

" What's it like up there this morning ? " he asked, glancing towards the sunshine on the slopes of Diphwys.

" Beautiful ! " we answered, not having seen it, but knowing it was never otherwise.

We had the train almost to ourselves, and the pleasures of a journey through the Halts without the drawback of having endured the discomforts of the twelve-five. As we passed it in one of the little stations, waiting to let us through, I gave it a dispassionate look. One would not have thought that we were old acquaintances.

At Chester we found that the motor-cycle, in the unaccountable manner of all machines, had gone wrong as it was having its final test, only half an hour before, and a new part would have to be sent for. Percy warned us that it was very old and looked it, but said that its engine was good. At the price it seemed surprising that it had an engine at all.

Back to Chester we went, and had just time to shop before running up that unpleasantly long road to the station. With a pair of kippers in one hand and a pair of Wellingtons in the other, my progress was considerably hampered by Mat, slithering about on the wet and greasy pavements in crêpe-soled shoes, making wild clutches at me when her feet slid beyond her control. The train was in, and we settled down to a long, slow journey. I revised my ancient knowledge by reading " The Two-stroke Engine." At the Halts the little oil-lamps were carefully collected and taken aboard, and we came at last to our own station—two hours late.

The air blew fresh from the sea. The night was clear and starry, and as we passed through the tollgate the keeper clanged and locked it for the night. We climbed the fence and reached the ditch where we had left the petrol, but the bottle had gone. We searched for ten minutes or so and gave it up, glad that we had brought only a quart instead of half a gallon. Perhaps the tide ran up and floated it out. If it had disappeared through human agency I was happy to think that someone was having trouble with oily plugs. I hoped it was raining and he had no torch.

Up the first hill the prospect of the three miles ahead was rather depressing, but by the time we had left the cluster of houses I was enjoying it. The heavens were high, vast and starry as we neared the mountains, and at half past one, when we reached our door, I could have walked all night.

THE KITCHEN, WITH FIRST ARM-CHAIR IN BACKGROUND, AND A
LATER ONE IN FOREGROUND

THE CHEST

A few days later the machine arrived at Penmaenpool, and I went down alone, with another bottle of petrol and oil mixture.

In the waiting-room was a very small Coventry Eagle, its frame apparently made from outsize pieces of Meccano. The signalman, who had left his box to attend to me, informed me that it was a girder frame. To have a machine with such a strong, such a solid-sounding foundation, was reassuring. Later, as I bounced in the air over the boulders, I was glad to think that I was bouncing on girders. Their very name inspires confidence. Suspension bridges and gigantic concrete buildings are founded on girders, but who builds on frail and hollow tubes?

I took the machine out to the side of the railway track and looked at it. Other people passing by looked too. It had a brilliant red tank, the paint obliterating all reference to its proud and high-sounding lineage. It might have been nobody's child. The red splash could be seen from half a mile away—a strange choice of colour, for it was certainly not the sort of machine to which one would want to draw attention. My only aim always has been to get by as unobtrusively as possible.

I pushed it along the road, out of sight of the station, and looked at it again. Percy was quite right—it was old. The saddle springs hung down from the side and the covering was ripped in several places, showing the stuffing beneath. Some time later the bullocks, in their eternal quest for a new taste, took the rest of the top and all the stuffing, but fortunately I retrieved it before it became cud, and stitched down what was left to a bit of canvas. There were no handle-bar grips, and the one-time twist-grip control had been replaced by a battered lever. Its decompressor was missing and the carburettor could be shaken about. The frame had been many times painted with a steadily thickening black, gritty paint. A hole in the back number-plate indicated where a rear light, if I had one, might go. Both mudguard tips seemed to have been gnawed away by rats. The exhaust pipe had been dented by many impacts, and a tangle of wires was tied to the handlebars with string. As assets, it had two very good brakes and powerful compression. The most magnificent and incongruous addition was a large shining fishtailed exhaust attached to the battered pipe ; but added to the general appearance, it simply looked like someone's error. The index letters of the number-plates were B.G. I looked at them thoughtfully and hoped it was, wondering, too, what a 1931 Coventry Eagle in its pristine beauty when first turned out by the manufacturers had looked like.

Taking off my shoes, I tied them together and slung them round my neck, putting on the Wellingtons instead. I poured in the contents of the petrol bottle and fiddled with the levers. I kicked it, and I went on kicking it, altering the throttle and ignition levers to try and find the magic spot that would bring it to life. Occasionally there was a stir somewhere inside the cylinder ; a vague promise to fire some time. But it was not ready yet. I alternately kicked it and ran with it in gear, and in course of time this brought me, exhausted, to near the end of the tollbridge road. Round the corner came one of those obliging youths who are always ready, even anxious, to get an obstinate engine to start. He, too, kicked it many times, and it responded to his kicks no better than it had to mine. Testing the plug by the bold method of grasping it as I kicked, he decided that it had life, and if pushed was bound to go. I was less certain. It is a statement so often made, and so rarely fulfilled, but I was willing to try, and putting it into gear, I got astride again. He pushed, and after a few yards, over which it dug in its heels and slid, like an obstinate puppy dragged on a lead, it suddenly surprised me and went. It gave a terrific roar and hurtled forward. I had neither the time nor the attention for thanks, but I hope the grateful attitude of my back did manage to convey some acknowledgment.

I warily crossed the main road, started up the lane, and having turned the corner by Evan Jones's garage, accelerated to get up the hill. As I passed between the high walls and the enclosing cottages I was ashamed of the noise I created on that peaceful afternoon. The only solution seemed to be to make still more noise in an attempt to go quicker and get out of earshot, but a very short experience of it showed me that although I could go faster, it was less easy to get out of earshot.

Climbing the next hill, I passed the chapel and swept round the bridge to the first gate. I put the gear lever in neutral and tried to tone down the engine to a gentle " pop-pop." Instead of responding, it gave a loud crescendo yell which vibrated through the valley, causing the petrol cap to leap off, and something inside the cylinder to rattle about alarmingly. The engine refused to be shut off. It worked to its fullest capacity, and nothing I could do would stop it. The piston went tearing up and down inside until I was afraid it would rupture itself.

I felt as helpless as the parent of a screaming child that refuses to be pacified, and tried to wrench off the loose carburettor. It was immovable. Frenzied, I unscrewed the top and pulled it off, and with a few final, tearing shudders, the noise stopped. Leaning the cycle against the bank, for it had no stand, I propped open the gate and pushed it through. Shutting the gate, I sat down to recover, then replaced the bits I had torn out and tried to start it. It was no use. It would not start, and kicking a motor-cycle with no decompressor is a tiring business. It then struck me that as it had started by being pushed I might manage again by getting on and letting it run down the hill. Propping open the gate, I turned round and started. I put it into gear, but it simply acted as a slight brake, and there we were at the bridge again like a depressing move in snakes and ladders.

This experience finally confirmed all I have ever felt about hills. It is a great mistake for the owners of decrepit vehicles to live at the top of them. They are tempted to run down them in the hope that their engines will fire, and when they don't, somehow or other, have to get them back to where they started.

It was this problem that faced me now. I sat on the railings for a long time, thinking that perhaps the engine needed to cool after its recent angry outburst. Every few minutes, I kicked it to show my displeasure. A long period followed, during which I left it there, climbed down into the little gorge, took off my Wellingtons, and sat with my feet in the stream, thinking.

I had to decide whether to take it down the second hill in the hope that it would fire, or make a superhuman effort to push it up the hill I had just come down, and somehow, sometime, get it home.

Weighing it all up, I decided on the second alternative, put on my boots, climbed to the road, and began. It was terribly hard work. I pushed for a yard or two, and held it stationary with the front brake until I regained strength and breath to go on. Halfway up, in anger, I gave it another feeble kick. It fired ! I got on quickly, sailed through the propped gate, regretfully leaving it open and hoping the cows would not stray too far. Near the brow, it showed another of its vices. A horrible, metallic rending noise began in the gearbox region, and we came almost to a stop, in spite of the determined-sounding engine. Alarmed, lest we stopped again, I leapt off and helped it to drag itself up the remaining slope. The Eagle struggled over the rise. On the level I leapt on again.

At the gates came the terrifying roar ; up the slopes, the alarming rend and leap off to keep the thing going. The journey began to be a nerve-shattering nightmare.

At the Isaf bridge, I could see from afar three figures sitting on the stone coping. One got off to hold the gate open. As I neared them, I saw they were three elderly men, and as I slowed to pass through the gate, I saw that they were all armed with little hammers. I looked again to make sure. It was so. The one who held the gate shouted :

" Have you seen any iron pyrites up here ? "

" No ! " I yelled back, rather dazed by the question.

" Thank you," he shouted, and

" Thank you " shouted I.

As I bumped along, I wondered whether they had really been there, really had hammers, really asked about iron pyrites. It was rather an extraordinary afternoon, for as I turned on to the forked track, I saw, in the sky above the Garn, a small barrage balloon floating all by itself up the valley. When I dared take my eyes off the rutty track, I looked again, almost expecting to see the three elderly men sitting on it. I should not have been greatly startled to see polar bears swimming in the stream that afternoon.

Up the last field, the bullocks galloped madly to the furthest corner as I appeared, their tails straight out behind them. The sheep ran in a wild flock, leaping the stone wall into the wood for safety.

Riding down the fields, I never needed to fear that bullocks would be lying on the track, or sheep scuttling through the gaps I was about to ride through. No horn, even had the Eagle owned one, was necessary. All animals regimented themselves in the furthest corners of the field as soon as the engine started, and even now, only the old residents are blasé ; the newly born, up to their first birthday or so, dash in terror, to get as far from the sound as possible. The next Easter, I think I caused a lot of premature births among the sheep. White dots appeared frequently and thickly after the Eagle had been out.

Sometimes on the way up, I'd find Bob Jones the postman, by the roadside waiting for me.

" I was away up in the hills as you went down," he would say. " Here is your post." Kath and Iolo could hear me as soon as I appeared on the brow of the hill, and often walked down to the chapel to catch me before I went by. The station master knew. Evan Jones knew. The Edwards at their farm high on the hillside above the track knew. It was as effective a way of announcing we were in residence as hoisting a flag. Probably more effective, for few would see the flag.

Its noise was terrifying, and until I became hardened to it, my heart, too, used to quicken in apprehension whenever it became necessary to kick that engine into life.

CHAPTER X

THE greater part of next morning was given up to finding out how to start the Eagle, and having found it, the quickest way of stopping her, but that we never really mastered.

I think that after being quiescent and lonely in the back of the house while we are away, the delight of hearing her own voice again runs away with her.

Her appearance, of course, one can do little for, and so long as she cruises along at a comfortable twenty miles an hour, showing that at least she works, I forget it. It is when she is stationary and intending to remain so that she is so striking. There is such a look of " I told you so ". The only justification for her existence is when she is in motion, and this was brought home to me very forcibly when I left her propped in a back street one day in Dolgelley, and returned to find two small boys gazing at her in silent wonder. " Does it *go* ? " they asked incredulously, as I prepared to mount. " Of course it does," I said. Even the Eagle was indignant, and produced two terrific backfires which awed them considerably. With honour vindicated, we banged slowly off up the street.

The morning after we got her, I rode up the mountain behind the house, so that Mat could give me an objective description of the rending noise. I returned to hear the diagnosis. " It sounds like anchor chain running through holes in biscuit tins ! "

A gearbox could, we supposed, sound like a biscuit tin under certain circumstances. We decided to have it off to discover what its circumstances were. Dismantling it took very little time. Most of it went in marvelling at the brain that invented so intricate a thing as a gearbox. The number of bits that came out of that small container astounded us. But we found no explanation of the noise, and started to fit the jigsaw together again. Everything went back except one small piece looking rather like the top of Britannia's trident, and this didn't seem to harmonize with the pieces already in. We tried it at every possible angle, and as the day went on I began to wonder whether we had picked up some small and unrelated bit of ironmongery from the scraps lying about.

We went doggedly on by the light of the pressure lamp, my persistence strengthened by the strong disinclination to do as I felt I might have to, that is, to take it to a Dolgelley garage and explain that it had fallen out ; could they please put it in again ?

At eleven o'clock, worn out and oily, we gave it up, pondering on ways and means of getting it fitted without losing too much face. Mat's last suggestion was that we should take the Eagle to the main road, and sit on the roadside with the trident in our hands, looking helpless until some passing motorist took pity on us. I turned this down, thinking of the Herculean task of pushing the inanimate hundredweights home again if we came back with the part still unfitted.

Like the theory of dovetails, the solution came to me in the night, and at the first attempt next morning the trident slipped into the cogs and spindles. So simple when one knows how : so utterly impossible when one has forgotten the way it came out.

One very curious thing resulted. Sometimes, on starting off, the Eagle goes *backwards*. So far it has only happened in low gear, and the thought that it might manifest itself at twenty miles an hour has often had a sobering effect on my driving.

Neither have I ever been able to cure its protesting roar at stops, and at the first hint that this is about to happen in public, I hurriedly go into gear again, and ride off to some obscure spot. Like being sick, it is a thing that one prefers to happen in private. My adopted system then, of turning off the petrol before reaching the shops, and cruising around the back streets until it ran out, became, after some practice, a game less of chance and more of skill, so that I know now exactly where the petrol must be turned off to bring me to a silent stop at the baker's.

The first trip down, I went prepared for all eventualities, a set of tools dropped into the top of my Wellingtons. These tools became the Eagle's vade mecum. Where the Eagle went, the tools went too. I had painted the tank with quick-drying Brunswick Black. It was hard and dry when I started. Unfortunately, as I soon discovered, petrol is an admirable solvent for Brunswick Black, and the jolts soon shook enough petrol through the filler cap to make a striking radial pattern in red and black down the sides of the tank. By the time I reached the shops a good deal of the pattern had transferred itself to my knees, and I was forced to walk from shop to shop in a slightly knock-kneed manner so as to hide it.

The tollbridge keeper, realizing in some intuitive way the peculiarities of the Eagle, flung open the gate wide, as in "John Gilpin," as soon as I appeared at the end of the bridge and with repetition, we have come to co-ordinate our movements very well. I have my toll fee ready, and he has the ticket, which I snatch like a relay runner as I pass by, thus inducing the Eagle to feel that since there is to be no stop, there is no need for noise.

I slowed up for a goods train that had just crept over the level crossing, expecting to receive the keeper's congratulations on shortening the long, long trail, but at the suggestion of a step the Eagle started that low, ominous sound that presages, very briefly, the nerve-shattering roar to follow. The signalman was opening the level crossing : I took the congratulations for granted and went.

As I rode down the narrow street into the town the volume of sound from the dilapidated exhaust pipe was thrown back from the tall buildings. The policeman on point duty turned his eyes on me from afar and, without a word, kept them fixed on me reprovingly as I passed in front of him. I slowed up in the market place and the roar threatened again. Shutting off the petrol, I headed up the Dinas road until it ran out. Half a mile out the engine died peacefully away, and I pushed it back again, suffering the commiserating looks usually given to those pushing motor cycles.

I felt a conspicuous figure. There was the appearance of the Eagle, and there was my own, with black striped knees.

So long as we sat together we looked more or less coherent and explained each other, but as soon as we parted the situation was different. I used to wish desperately that the creature was tractable enough to ride from shop to shop, so that outside each stood the reason for my appearance, for proprietor and customer to see. But I could never be sure of her behaviour, and the only safe way was to leave her and shop on foot. Since the Eagle entered our household my shopping habits have changed. I patronize mostly the small, obscure shops in the out of the way streets.

It was during this holiday that we first met Bob Huw, a cat left behind by earlier Canol occupants, who had gone just before we took Blaen-y-cwm. For years he went semi-wild, his faith in human nature destroyed. Then gradually he adopted us, entering the house slyly, by the open windows, rarely by the door, drinking the milk and eating the scraps we left for him in the hall. As his trust returned he became bolder, and sat on the hearthrug in the evening, large, impassive and tiger-like, but ever ready to leap for liberty if we became too familiar. Someone seemed to have taught him that " The price of Liberty is Eternal Vigilance," and he made it quite clear that we were the favoured and the inferiors : he would make all the running. Through the holidays he stayed with us, unfettered, coming and going as the fancy moved him, leaving suddenly and stalking into the dark night with a wild look in his eye, returning next day smug and satisfied.

That cat had a memory and a pride, for although he would follow us down the fields to the Canol bridge, running ahead and waiting for us in the rushes, yet beyond the bridge on to Canol terrain he refused to set foot. It was as though he said, " They wronged me : I shall never cross their threshold again."

The day preceding our going a restlessness became apparent. He walked from room to room with his tail in the air, and then, suddenly, he was gone. It was as if the upheavals of packing stirred in his memory and opened old sores. He gave us no chance of deserting him ; he always deserted us first.

One holiday he failed to appear. We missed him ; we
had liked his trustful and impersonal acceptance of our hos-
pitality, and his confidence that it would be unchanged when
we came again.   For days we expected him, leaving windows
open , and calling at dusk into the shadows of the wood and
towards the rocks of the Garn, " Bob Huw ! Bob Huw ! "
But he never came again, and long after Richard Jones found
him dead in the barn.

By now all three bedrooms were reasonably habitable, but
the plywood tea-chest covering the hole in the ceiling of the
bedroom we had not yet used offended our æsthetic sense, so
we took it down, hoping to be able to fill in the gap with
plaster.   We found that the laths and anchorage underneath
were rotted away, and had to fix new ones.   The plaster we
mixed to cover them was a curious sort of pottage—of agri-
cultural lime, Blaen-y-cwm sand, bits of sheeps' wool, chopped
hair from the armchair cushions, and very fine wood shavings
which I manufactured specially for the purpose.   All this,
we hoped, would enable it to hang together.   The ceiling
with this patch of stucco hardly looked an entity, but it
pleased us better than stencilled tea-chest ; and when it still
stayed up after three days we felt it would be safe to distemper it.

But odd happenings dated from the first time the room was
slept in.   Anne, Arnold and Toni had come to stay with us,
and on two violins and a 'cello practised Dohnanyi and Bach
that evening, while Mat and I sat on the sun-warmed slab
under the holly skeleton and listened to the notes floating out
into the still evening, until the midges and chill of the mountain air sent us in again.   We went to bed late and Anne
and Arnold slept in the repaired bedroom.   About two
o'clock in the morning they woke us, softly opening our door
and asking us, in whispers, to come and listen to an odd noise
in the ceiling.   Rather startled we got out of bed, tiptoed
across the landing, and sat on their bed for several quiet
minutes, waiting.   Nothing happened.   We went back to
bed, and had just fallen asleep when they woke us again.
We returned.   After a short time it began.   It was a curious
noise ; a constant processing between the plastered hole to

the ceiling above the door and back again. It sounded like a smallish creature walking with great care and deliberation in smallish hobnailed boots. The steps were very regular and so were the journeys, with a few seconds' stop at each end before turning round and coming back. We wondered whether we had perhaps walled up some living creature ; but why it wore boots we could not understand. In any case it was not a very likely explanation. The plaster had been up too long for anything there to be still living, and the steps sounded too regular and mechanical to be made by anything alive. No explanation was really satisfactory. After a quarter of an hour it stopped, and we all went to bed again. It came back at intervals through the night, but there was nothing we could do about it.

A few days later, as we sat at supper, the unlatched kitchen door was gently scraped and pushed open, and as gently drawn to again. Since it never moves of its own accord, however windy the day, we could think of no explanation of this either. When, the same night, a large apple pie disappeared from the top of the dairy cupboard without trace, and without breakage of any of the crockery placed precariously round it, we gave up trying to think of explanations.

Various other strange things happened. Lamps, which had hitherto been safe to leave lit and turned low, would be turned high and smoking when we came back to them. Once the Rippingille either lit itself, or was lit by the creature. Books left face downwards were at a different page when we picked them up, although we had not touched them in the meantime. One night we were suddenly wakened by " Knock ! knock ! " on the floor directly beneath our beds. I picked up a shoe and answered with " Knock ! knock ! " but the conversation stopped. Next night we heard through the open window a sound of heavy steps and scrapings on the doorslab. In the still and peaceful air they sounded extraordinarily loud. No horses were grazing in our fields at the time, and the sound was too heavy for unshod animals. We put our heads out of the window and Mat called, " There's no one at home. Go away." Nothing answered, but it obligingly went.

Before we locked the door next night we looked out at the stars, and as I turned towards the southern sky I saw in the first field the sudden glimmer of a lantern just beyond our gate. It was quite still, casting its little circle of light on the path by the trees. It seemed odd.

" I expect Willie or his father are up looking at the sheep," I said.

" But it's very late," answered Mat. " They are never up so late as this. And anyhow they'd need the lamp—they wouldn't leave it there."

" Shall we go round to the barn and see ? " I asked, hoping she would feel as unwilling as I.

" No," she said quickly, as she prepared to shut the door. " We can ask to-morrow—but I don't think it's likely, some-how."

Nor was it, for next day we asked and no one had been up at all. The lamp was gone.

Strangely enough these events were not frightening. The feeling of being safely behind a two-inch elm door was com-forting, though as Mat pointed out, IT also was probably safe behind the locked door with us. But time had given us the feeling of being familiar with the house, and the impres-sion that it was a friendly one. So was the valley, and our neighbours dotted about in it. We had a conviction that nothing very untoward could happen in that peaceful place.

There must be some simple explanation, but we have never found it. Had each happening been separate and isolated in time from the rest we should have probably for-gotten about them after a passing surprise.

Our friends went, and that night there was one last occur-rence when we thought it was taking a final farewell by bringing the house about our ears.

I suddenly found myself sitting bolt upright in bed and saying to Mat, " What was that ? " She had also been instantaneously wakened by it—a heavy bouncing of the bedroom floor, jerking the beds and giving me the feeling one gets in dreams—of falling suddenly out of a tree. After a few seconds there was a deep, far-away rumble, repeated later in the night, with another bounce. We decided " Earthquakes," and went to sleep, relieved that our creature was not, at any rate, responsible for this. But our earthquakes were scoffed at in the valley next day. No one had heard or felt anything of it.

For the first time I began to feel a trifle disturbed. A small something wearing hobs, eating apple pie amd playing with lanterns was one thing ; a creature big enough and vindictive enough to try to bounce us out of bed was another. We kept all the lamps between our beds at night, in case it grew careless, and scoured the house each evening with the hurricane lamp before we went to sleep.

Later that week we were at Kath's idly looking at an old newspaper lying on the table and read, in a paragraph tucked away on the back page, that our neighbouring county had experienced an earth tremor at the same time on the same night as we had been wakened. We breathed easily again, grateful that at least one disturbance was explained, and when we came again all was peaceful. Perhaps, like us, it had felt that an adversary which can shake a house is too powerful to live with.

We had no sooner forgotten the earthquake when we had a cloud-burst. It came on a dull and lowering afternoon with an unnaturally dark sky and gusts of wind. Suddenly there was a loud clatter of hailstones on the thick glass slab of the stairs skylight, and the ground was quickly covered in them, the size of sloes. They bounced on the grass like tennis balls, and soon the landscape was pure white. The sky changed from grey to an ominous yellow, and the hail to rain—rain of such intensity that its sibilance filled the house, and all the hollows in the first field which hold a pool of water after a day's rain were full in a few minutes.

It poured off the broken gutter and cascaded in front of the window like a curtain. We raced quickly round the house to find our vulnerable points. The roof, thank heaven, stood up to it, but the gully behind the house had filled, and water was gushing through the dry stone walling into the dairy and the two other back places. In the middle one it was over ankle depth and rising quickly. I rushed round to see whether we could divert it, but there was no hope there.

At the back of the house a solid sheet of water poured down the slope and emptied itself into our gully. Boiling and bubbling, it endeavoured to force a way out by the old water-wheel outlet, and finding it too slow, it was of necessity taking a short cut through the house. The bog too was an amazing sight, for the whole area between the stile and the wood was a white and seething mass of water, tearing down with a speed, ferocity and volume increased beyond anything we could ever have imagined there. I fetched Mat out to see the unusual sight of high waves leaping into the little wood. As I looked again at the gully I felt rather as Canute must have done. There was nothing we could do to stop it. The most we could hope to manage was to assist it as quickly as we could through the house.

We took buckets and baled, running to the front door and flinging the water down the slope, but the wind blew in more, and blew back as much as it could of what we flung out, and worse, the water inside was gaining on us. When it began trickling over the door sill into the hall, I felt that more drastic measures were needed, and lifting down the heavy woodman's axe, I knocked the sill away. We took brooms, and working one behind the other, swept the water along the hall and out at the front, working furiously as we got there, in a losing battle with the wind. I have no idea how long we spent pushing the flood through the house. When at last it seemed to be welling up with less speed, and we had time to straighten our backs, mine felt as though it had been bent for a very long time.

Near dusk, the rain stopped, and we took the can and started off for the milk. The bottom field was entirely under water, and as far as we could see down the valley, a tossing expanse of waves carried down a swirling wreckage of tree roots, branches, fence posts, mats of rushes and torn-up heather roots.

We waded slowly to the bridge, currents from all directions eddying over the tops of our Wellingtons. In the shallower parts, the green grass, swaying in the vagaries of the flow, streamed out like smoothly combed emerald hair. Two of the big stone monoliths of the bridge had been battered by the wreckage and forced into the water. For once, I was glad that we had come by train, for there was no way out of the field for a car except by the bridge. The flood stretched up the Canol lane, and the track above was torn into great gullies exposing boulders deep down, pale and sickly looking from long burial. Where the slope lost its steepness, debris had been dropped in sudden weariness, and lay in a long mound across the way. We climbed over it, thankful again that we had come by train.

By next morning, it had begun to strike us that we had witnessed an unusual sort of phenomenon, and it might be just as well to descend to the bigger world to see its results. Devastation was similar the whole length of the valley, but at the bottom of the first hill, its force must have been gigantic, for the old stone bridge was completely gone. The water roared through a steep and rocky gully, with no vestige of a way across. A bridge might never have been. Awed, we gazed into the chasm and then turned and went home.

For days, each time we went out, we had more news of the damage, and then the valley settled back into its old routine. Crossing the mainstream to get to the bottom, before a temporary span of planks was made, was a matter of finding shallows to wade, and gullies narrow enough to jump, and when we came again, the lovely old stone bridge by the chapel was replaced by a utility structure with fenced sides.

I was filling the kettle at the waterfall one day soon after the cloudburst, and hearing the long bird-like whistles, wild cries and barks, which indicate that Richard Jones is sheep gathering, I waited for him to appear round the corner of the house to tell him that a cup of tea would soon be ready.

Looking at the great iron kettle I held, he said, " It would not be much trouble to bring water into the house."

Remembering recent events, I thought, " No trouble at all,"—but as he went on to say, " A small tank by the wall you could have, and the pipes down through the dairy window. I have done the same at my own house," his meaning awned on me.

Thinking it over, we also decided it would be possible to bring water into the house, and better still, to send it out again by way of the water wheel gully ; and then putting the idea into cold storage, we got on with more essential things.

Next time we went to shop, the Canol, the empty farm beyond our bridge, was occupied. We were amazed to see the door open and evidence of great upheavals within. Two blank-looking faces appeared at the door, and asked us the time. We hated them—for taking the Canol, for wanting to know the time, and for their blank faces. But when the Canol still looked itself, we began to feel, rather cautiously, that since they hadn't ruined the house, they were not, perhaps, so awful as we had imagined. By now, we know we could not have kinder or more helpful neighbours. Their faces have ceased to be blank. Perhaps we too looked blank at that first meeting. Their amazement was at seeing two people apparently rise up from the river like Joseph's seven lean kine, when they had imagined their house was the last in the valley and they the highest inhabitants.

They had ladders—beautiful, long, light extending ones. They lent them to us. They did more—they helped us. The merest suggestion that the thought of the morrow's work lay heavy on our minds was enough to send two of them up soon after crack of dawn in working-trousers, with cigarettes in every pocket, at a time when we could only get Mannikins.

Unless one has been in our position, with the only available ladders a mile off, of immense weight, rotten and worm-eaten withal, it is difficult to grasp the significance of the existence of a light extending one a few fields away. It eased our repairs enormously. We scampered over the roof at a much accelerated rate. Since then, we have added war surplus Accles and Pollock steel scaling ladders to our equipment, and little by little are becoming self-supporting in roof repair equipment.

When we had time to get round to the idea of bringing water into the house, we asked the skilled workers of the Canol what they thought of it. They thought well of it.

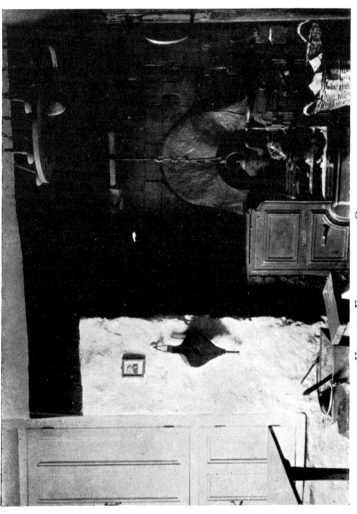

Kitchen Fireplace and Chandelier

THE BOG

THE BOG WITH CLOUDBURST

In half an hour, it was all planned. Better than plans was an indication that we could call on them to put in the tap and do all the inside plumbing.

The large earthenware pipes were delivered to the Canol, and we let it be known among our friends, that anyone visiting us would be expected to pick up a drainpipe on the way and bring it up. I still see in my mind's eye, several figures, each bearing a large earthenware pipe on their shoulder, looking in the evening light extraordinarily like smugglers as they passed in single file along the wall of the last field, bent heads and pipes casting long shadows across the quiet fields.

Whitsuntide came, and the days were long. We started work. The plan was to submerge the pipes in the stream as far as the wall separating us from the mountain, for the height was enough to give sufficient pressure to bring the water through. We dammed the stream, diverting it to the bog. Even so, it was hard to get rid of all the trickles, and we worked constantly in pebbly, peaty pools. To get the pipe line as straight as possible meant digging out many large boulders, and I began to have some inkling of what Sisyphus must have felt, for often, when we had got one precariously poised on its axis, we would slip, and the thing would settle firmly back into its bed, with a satisfied squelch. Uprooting rushes was almost as bad. Their evil-smelling roots went deep into the peaty bed, and clung there tenaciously. With pickaxe, fork and crowbar, we hacked and levered at them from all sides, and then, as we tugged at their speared stems, they would suddenly release their hold in a churlish manner, and we would stagger drunkenly back down the slope, clutching the wet mass.

The midges were particularly vicious around the stream. They seemed to find the paraffin we had dabbed on our faces pleasant to the taste. On the third day, as we struggled among the roots in the dusk, bitten on eyelids, face and ears, Mat suddenly straightened herself, and leaning on her spade said, in the quiet, savage tones of one maddened beyond endurance,

" Has it ever struck you that we come here for a holiday ?

We spend the whole of daylight, digging and delving ; we work longer than we should ever consider it possible at home, we work every day, we work like navvies, and when we go upstairs to bed, we are so exhausted we are already asleep."

It had not struck me before, but now it was put to me so forcibly, I began to wonder whether a tap was really necessary. Why were we cumbering ourselves with this trapping of civilization when we might be on the mountains. I, too, became conscious of blisters and aches, midges and cut hands.

We went in, and I dreamt all night long that our damming of the stream had flooded the valley, and caused a devastation more vast than that of the cloudburst.

As we sat over a leisurely breakfast, balance was restored. We took our time, and we delved only when we felt like it.

At last, the course was laid. The opening of the Sukkur dam cannot have given greater satisfaction to its engineers than our few pipes gave us. When they were all in place, I looked at them, and thought with immense respect of the mind which directed the laying of the Cwm Dyli pipeline. How had they got them so straight ? How had they avoided the bends and turns, and ups and downs we seemed to have got into ours ? Above all, how had they gone on doing it in their miles-long stretch ? This poor little line zig-zagged and dipped all over the place, and as for cementing the pipes together, it was all but impossible to get to the lower halves of their joints. After failing many times, we consoled ourselves for these inadequacies by reflecting that as they were actually in the stream bed, if the water ran out of their joints, it would just as easily run in.

The Canol people brought up a second-hand sink, a tap, and a length of piping that looked like a large coiled ophicleide. We fetched it all up in the cart, and prepared for the culmination of our labours—the inside plumbing. The skilled labour arrived ; the casual labour sat down and looked on.

They started to take down the dairy wall. Willie, who was up to see to the sheep, remarked placidly,

" The wall will come down. Just like it did before. The

crack is still plain to see where we built it up," and then seeing my expression,

" You need have no fear. I will stand by here and hold it up. If it is too heavy," he added, with a twinkle. " You are both grown used to putting back the old slates, and it will not be so very different."

We went in. I found it difficult to watch without trepidation, and judging from Mat's apprehensive look, so did she. I stood with a calm and confident air for as long as I could, but when they started levering out the big rocks under the window, I anxiously waited for the dust to settle, so that I could assure myself that we still had four walls. When we could actually see the view outside through a gaping hole by the water wheel, I felt that the last straw had been removed and it was only a matter of minutes to the collapse. I could endure it no longer, and we went to safety outside.

We sat there in a depressed way, cleaning the sink with spirits of salt.

" I wonder how long it will take to rebuild if it does fall," said Mat gloomily.

" We shan't try to rebuild it," said I, firmly. " We'll just shut it up and live in the rest of the house. There'll be less roof to mend."

After a time the crashes stopped and we stole back to see what had happened. There was the comforting sound of wet cement being slapped on. The house was being put together again. The tap was in place, and a neat brick platform lay ready to receive the sink. By afternoon it was finished ; we had only to wait for the cement to dry before we turned on the tap.

Next morning the dairy had a large pool of water on the floor. My worst fears were realized. The roof must have been shaken by yesterday's events, and developed new leaks. I spent two hours crawling over it, cementing up any likely looking cracks.

At midday we decided that the cement was hard enough for the ceremonial opening, and I went outside to build up the little pool that was to be our storage reservoir. Mat, with lordly pomp, released the dam we had made. The water flowed down with great deliberation, filling each tiny runnel and hollow before turning its attention to the next one. We strolled alongside, and went in for the culminating moment of harnessing the vast resources of the Blaen-y-cwm spring, and guiding it through our little tap.

The tap had anticipated us ; water was pouring through it into the sink, down the waste pipe and back to the stream. It didn't matter, it was just as satisfactory ; though there was a feeling that the ship had slid down the slipway when our back was turned, and without the champagne. It did explain one thing, and that was the wet floor, for the tap had been open all night, and the night's rain had been sufficient to fill the reservoir and run through the tap with enough force to splash over on to the floor.

" Bringing water into the house " was a great labour saver, though like other houses with mod. cons., it has its drawbacks. In hard winters, the lead pipe from the course to the tap freezes and bursts, so that now it has numerous leaks, but since they are all outside, there is no call to do anything about it, for our little spring has never been known to run dry.

All it needs is a yearly clearance of water weed from its higher reaches. On the way up we keep a look out for drowned lambs, for near the mountain it is deep, and a lamb following its foolish mother can easily fall in. After winter's storms, it is sometimes necessary to blow hard up the tap before it will run. When one has stopped blowing, it is best to remove one's mouth quickly before the few worms preserved in peaty water trickle through, and then it resumes its usual clear flow.

To celebrate our tap, we took the Canol tenants out to dinner at the most opulent of the local hotels. We went down in their car, on their small petrol ration, and ate steadily through all that appeared, and after a toast to the Blaen-y-cwm spring we started home along the estuary road. This was our first journey up the valley with head-lights. It was wet and dark ; very wild, but beautiful. The silver birches stood out against a background of wet red bracken, there was a constantly moving pattern of shadows as the lights fell upon trunks, hedges and gateposts, and in the sheltered corners, sudden clusters of brilliant, staring eyes of sheep caught in the glare. Lovely as it was, I should not have cared for this to be my first journey. There was an indescribable wildness about the scene as we crossed the bridge, and the headlights, through the spears of rain, swept across the mountain as we turned to the bog, to find a flooded track. Had I been one of my own visitors, I would have leapt out of the car after the first lurch over the bridge, and at the sight of the desolation beyond would have chosen the lonely walk down the valley and a bed in Dolgelley. As we slithered up the lane a mountain hare leapt out of a clump of rushes, and loped along in the brilliant light, to vanish in the fields towards the top wood.

I remember that, in gratitude, we moved a hundred bricks for the Canol, in our little cart, in half mile trips, up a gradient of one in three. It was one of the heaviest morning's work I have ever done, but small enough return for the pleasures of a tap.

The Canol continued to be a constant support when our ideas outran our abilities. Furthering them one day, the skilled labour rolled most of the way down our back roof, but, fortunately, we managed to field him before he went over the edge.

Surprised at the way their kindness persisted, even after such mishaps, I suggested to Mat that perhaps we were quite nice people for this to have gone on for so long a time Mat's answer was brief and disillusioning.

" No," she said, brusquely. " It's only that they are."

CHAPTER XI

IN the war years, we had spent most of one term in air raid shelters and in conversations down there, I had discovered several fishing enthusiasts. The boys spent their Sundays, they told me eagerly, in the Essex gravel pits catching perch, which they brought home and kept in tin baths. What happened to them after that I could never rightly make out.

It led me to wonder—why had we never thought of fishing at Blaen-y-cwm. If we could catch fish and make our own bread we should rarely need to do much shopping. Then I forgot about it until one day when I was casually looking through the school library and came across a book on rod-making.

The writer recommended timbers of whose names I had never heard, nor could I find a merchant who stocked them. I had to make do with a licence-free length of hornbeam, and a heavier and more cross-grained piece of timber I have never met.

I made it into a fourteen-foot perch pole and fitted it with shining brass rings. When it was finished, I found that perch do not live in mountain streams, or at least, not in our mountain stream. Even if they had, they would have been safe from me. Wielding the fourteen feet of hornbeam was as physically exhausting as, I should imagine, is tossing the caber. It was quite useless, unless, perhaps, it had been given cannon mountings and fixed in the stern of some large boat for tunny fishing.

I changed to the lighter labour of a ten-foot trout rod in ash. It tapered gracefully to an eighth of an inch, and made a whistling, whippy noise as I tried it. Looked at from the side, it was straight and handsome, but peered along from end to end, it snaked about like a mountain track.

When it was finished, I visited an elegant tackle shop in the neighbourhood of Piccadilly to buy flies. The customers seemed to be not of the kind who catch perch in gravel pits on Sundays, and keep them in tin baths, nor did I feel that the assistants were familiar with fishing of that kind. The young man who glided forward at my approach looked as though he was simply passing time here between one fishing week-end and the next on his own estate, and my first mistake so upset him that he found it hard to give me his full attention.

He asked me whether I wanted wet or dry flies. Now, although I knew that some people buy bathing costumes to get wet in and some people buy them as mere beach wear, and that the two costumes and the two buyers are often quite unlike, I did not know that there was the same sort of distinction between fishermen and the flies they bought, and I implied by my answer that as all my flies would be wet quite soon, it didn't really matter which kind I had now. They looked similar enough in all conscience.

Apparently their differences were vast. I read all I could on wet and dry flies, and the writers had one common conviction—that worm fishers were the lowest of the low. The intricacies, etiquette and traditions of the game discouraged me. Some anglers, apparently, went out with a small spring balance, and after meticulously weighing each catch and noting down all the circumstances attending its capture, threw it back in the river.

I had no intention of doing this, if ever I caught anything. It was on too high a plane—an ideal I could never strive for. My approach was purely utilitarian ; to catch fish by fly, worm, tickling or poaching so that we could *eat* them. No one, in the books, mentioned eating them, and I began to feel that to want to do so denoted some form of cannibalism.

The more I read, the more vast and complicated the subject became. I bought a little book looking like a wad of bus tickets fastened together, and when one flicked over its pages quickly, there was a graceful representation of " Fisherman Casting." A note at the end told me that I could have lessons in the art for a guinea.

Balance was restored by Willie.

" How do you catch trout ? " I asked him. " Do you use flies ? "

" Not often," he said. " I just drop my worm into a good place when the weather is right. It must not be a cold day, and you must not let the fish see you. Creep—creep all the time."

One warm day soon after this, I assembled the rod, dug my worms, and went upstream to a big pool with a waterfall at its head, a huge boulder at the foot, behind which I could keep out of sight, and a great oak leaning out into the stream in which I could entangle my hook. Because of midges and cigarette shortages I took also a clay pipe bought in Barmouth, and an ounce of " Digger " tobacco.

Insects were thick above the water. Had I been less ignorant I should perhaps have identified them as a hatch of Mayfly. After using almost half a box of matches, I had the pipe well started. I flung in my worm and waited expectantly, and was faintly surprised, but not despondent, when I drew it out without a fish. A large one must surely live in that pool, I argued, and getting it was only a matter of patience.

My expectations had been coloured by my recent reading. " The reel screamed as the four-pounder darted for the overhang of the rock." The rock behind which I stood had a deep overhang, and the water beneath it was four or five feet deep, but the big four-pounder made no dart for it, nor did it even look at my worm. The reel did not scream, and it took me some years to realize that in these lively and tumbling little mountain streams, it never would. A rapid, but gentle unwinding, is the most that has ever been demanded of it. My landing net now serves for carrying potatoes. I am glad I stopped short of buying a gaff. Flies, both wet and dry, lie rusting in a tin box, and a line-drier, given to me one birthday, has been turned to other uses. My line dries, the few yards of it that are wet, by whistling and waving in the wind as I walk back from the mountain.

I stayed at the pool for about an hour, gently and persistently dropping the worm into as many eddies as I could reach. Any attempt to cast simply entangled the hook in the tree, and I spent as much time in climbing the tree to free it, and wading the pool to disentangle it from rusty wire and rotting fence posts, as I did in waiting for the trout to notice my worm. When patience began to wear thin, I decided that he had probably gone upstream to sun himself in open water and followed him.

I tried all the pools for half a mile, and then the clay pipe, efficient enough for its intended purpose, began to give me a curious feeling of having a balloon in my chest which inflated itself with every breath. I lay down flat in the bracken and gazed at the sky, and when the sky began to spin slowly round, I shut my eyes and dozed.

When I woke to the sound of nearby bleating sheep, the sun had moved far to the west. Feeling better, I lay looking into the deep brown pool below. The pipe I put away, deciding the cure was worse than the disease. Beneath, in the deepest channels of the stream, I could see shoals of fish, the biggest of them perhaps nine inches long. I know now that he is the biggest I shall ever catch, and then only on my lucky days. Collecting my tackle, I walked slowly home to explain, as many fisherman have done, that I had caught nothing.

I tried again many times, with the same result, and after constant failures ceased to expect anything. I took the rod out merely as an excuse to ramble about the streams. Remembering Rat's remark in *The Wind in the Willows* to the effect that nothing came up to just messing about in boats, I felt that messing about in streams without a boat was an equally good way of spending an afternoon.

For hours, I lay watching the elusive spotted trout in still and sunlit water, or wading from pool to pool and waterfall to waterfall under the dark, overhanging trees of summer days. Life on days like this had a dreamlike quality. Time was of no account. Mat tried fishing, too, but gave it up after one day, and succumbed to the charm of wandering, without the encumbrance of a rod.

We found a mallard's nest, and saw grey wagtails and dippers. In the quiet length of water, weed-grown and still where it slides from the lake before embarking on its mad rush down the valley, we found white and yellow water-lilies, and sinister, still peat hags, deep enough to drown in. In late summer the lake cwm was a sweep of heather. Earlier, scores of gulls nested there, a flock of brilliantly white birds, each on a little raft of rush on the dark expanse of water. One of them had lazily not bothered to go to the trouble of making a raft, feeling safe enough in this remote place, and had simply laid her eggs on a few washed-up rushes lying on the stone causeway across the lake. Her screeches of anger when she had to rise, as we scrambled from rock to rock and drew nearer, were full of incredulous amazement that such a thing could happen to her.

On the higher, open moor, wheatears and meadow pipits flitted ahead of us from wall to wall, and on the craggy cliffs stonechats flew from the heather in agitation, with their sharp call sounding so much like pebbles shaken in a bag. We found the nest of a pipit or Gwas-y-Gog—Cuckoo's servant, as the Welsh have named it. Ring-ousels still nested in Craig-y-Deryn. Raven, buzzard and carrion crow wheeled silently into the sky from the upper cwm while we were yet far away, and each with distinctive cry sailed majestically above until we had gone from sight.

On the slopes of Diphwys we came across a beautiful little shepherd's hut, built of boulders. Inside, a slab of rock formed the fireplace and two large slabs rearing skywards had been left to serve as a chimney. Others made seats near the fireplace. It was within a stone's throw of the track up which we had been so often and yet was so hidden and merged into the surroundings that one could pass within ten yards of its door and see it merely as a pile of naturally lying rocks.

At dusk, as we returned by the lake on still evenings, we sometimes saw huge fish leap from the water, but this always happened at the time of day when the simpler attractions of our own lower cwm appealed more strongly than the awesome beauty of the dark sombre slopes stretching to the water and mirrored there. We used to give one quick look at the wonderful sweeping shapes and the motionless black

water, and, fish or no fish, turn for home. To try to catch
fish there at dusk seemed like sacrilege, and would probably
have brought a stern punishment from the deity guarding it.

On one of these days of wandering I caught my first fish—
almost by accident, for I had dropped my rod in an absent-
minded fashion into a brown roaring spate after heavy rain.
By teatime we had a bagful. Since then, when I set out to
catch fish, I frequently bring some home, none more than
nine inches long, but none so small that decency demands
they should be thrown back.

But why one can catch fish one day and not the next I
cannot understand, and as far as I can gather from the
writers of fishing books, neither can they.

The spate fell and left our reservoir blocked, and in clearing
it I stubbed my bare toes hard on an upstanding rock. I
stood on one leg, agonized, unable to so anything but clutch
my injured foot with both hands. It was several days before
I could bear anything on my feet, and as soon as I could
manage to, I went down to shop. Before I had travelled
more than three fields, my stubbed toes began to feel red hot.
I stopped and took off my boot to see whether they had
become incandescent, but to my disappointment they looked
fairly normal. I filled my Wellington with water and put it
on again. For a short time it felt better, but soon the water
seemed to have reached boiling point. I emptied it out and
refilled it each time the track passed near the stream, and
before I crossed the tollbridge I filled it once more from a
spring, hoping that its coolness would last out until my
return.

In Dolgelley, I wished I had chosen to endure the red-hot
toes. It was impossible to walk without loud squelchings and
splashings. I left a wet right footprint on the pavement
wherever I walked. On the other hand, I did not want to
add to other oddities by taking off my boot in public and
pouring a pint of water into the gutter. My toes grew hotter
and hotter, and I was thankful indeed when I reached the
valley bottom and could fill up again in the stream below
Enid's house.

Enid was leaving her farm this year, and we went over to

have tea with her there for the last time. Most years she had
a so-called pet lamb, whose mother had either died or not had
enough to feed it. They lived in the kitchen and were bottle-
fed, lying in a little basket by the fire, hardly able to stand, and
protected from the draughts by pieces of old blanket.

This year she had three, grown large enough to gambol,
and tea was a hilarious sort of meal, where small children,
dogs, kittens, cats, puppies and lambs chased each other
interminably round the kitchen, as happy and easy with
each other as though they were all of the same species. The
curly haired lambs joined in with the greatest abandon.
They had none of the air of the traditional orphan. When
chased, they leapt for the open staircase and the landing, and
peeping round the edge of the newel-post, looked down at us
impishly.

By summer they had lost their grace and become fat adoles-
cents, and ran to meet us like old friends as we passed. A
further year's growth and they became matronly, and behaviour which had been attractive in them as lambs became
foolish in adults. They scurried up behind, gave us a kittenish
sort of push and tripped along with us. It was the equivalent,
in a sheep, of dotage in a person.

One such had been brought up with the rest to graze with
the Blaen-y-cwm flock, but it was a weak, poor thing, and
looked ill from the start.

" I have dosed it," said Willie, " but it seems no better ;
I think it will die."

It hung about our little enclosure, listless, with drooping
head, too weary to move even when we were only a step
from it, and it lay by the holly stump as though anxious not
to be too far from human aid when its time came. It died
when we were all far from home on top of Cader, sitting with
our feet over the edge of the great Bard's Chair, looking
towards our valley and discussing whether we should descend
the way we had come, from the south, or down Fox's Path,
and across country to the tollbridge. I was all for prospecting a new way, avoiding lakes, for my friends had alarmed me,
the only poor swimmer, by plunging into Llyn Cau, before
we scrambled to the summit by the short cut at the head of it.

As they struck out into that black water and slowly swam out until they were far beyond any hope of my rescuing, I thought of all the sinister stories I had heard of drownings in mountain pools ; cramped by the icy chill, dragged down by hidden currents. The thought of losing four friends at one blow was unbearable, and I turned away. When I looked again I was immeasurably thankful to see them turn for the shore. They clambered out, shivering, telling me how cold it was ; and I was very glad, and hoped they would remember it when we next came to a lake.

When we got home the poor sheep lay dead on the door-step. She was still warm, and I wished we had been a little earlier to give her, perhaps, some feeling of support. It was a very hot evening, and we decided we must move her quickly. We put her on an old door and carried her, rather sadly, to the dark coolness of the barn, sending the news to Richard Jones, and wondering where he, in his turn, would take her. He came up next day, when we were out, and as we sat out-side before supper a curious and unpleasant smell kept wafting by on the sunset breeze.

Assuming the sheep to be safely interred, it puzzled us. Next morning it was even stronger and floated in through the open windows as we lay in bed. It suddenly stirred a forgotten memory. I remembered a similar smell, years ago ; a dead rat under the sitting-room floorboards. Recalling the intensity of that smell from one small rat, I thought of the size of the sheep, and then, getting out of bed, went round to the barn. It was as I feared ; the stench increased ; I held my nose, pushed open the door and peered in. There it lay, swollen and horrible, with maggots swarming over it. Return-ing, I shut the windows and we went out again for the day. The evening air, on our return, was thick and heavy with it, and we carried on behind closed doors and windows, as in a barricaded fortress.

In the next move of the dead sheep, I always think that I acted with the greatest nobility. At dawn I arose, leaving the others asleep, and taking a rope, went out and tied it with superhuman will power, to the door. The object it bore was no longer recognizable as a sheep. I dragged the swollen, stinking mass to the very end of the green lane, where I left it and fled, and with no compunction at all, I drank the whole of our remaining brandy before breakfast. I needed it, for the thing had burst before the journey's end.

"A change of air is what you need," said Mat, kindly. "What about getting the week's shopping in the mild, soft climate of Dolgelley?"

I went, filling the rucksack so full that I was compelled to carry the joint, a loaf, a cake and a packet of Cornflakes on the tank. It was simple enough on the main road, but at the bend by the railed bridge, the loaf bounced off into the cataract below. But water, despite its apparent seethe and hurry, is often deceptively slow. It rushes madly, but it may not get anywhere, at least not very far, and even that in a sluggardly manner. I kept a wary eye on the loaf as I propped the Eagle against the posts of the bridge. It had shot swiftly down the first waterfall, but as soon as it reached the first deep pool it circled slowly and lazily round, and I seized it before it had the chance to shoot the next rapid. Evan Jones was passing on his tractor as I lifted it, wet and dripping, from the water.

"Bake it," he shouted, with a wide grin. "Put it in the oven like as if you were baking proper bread. It will make a new loaf."

At the next gate the pile on the tank seemed smaller. I checked it over and found the cake was missing. Hurriedly I rode back to find it. Face downwards in the middle of the track, there it was in its burst paper bag, and there also was a fat and motherly Buff Orpington clucking with delight as she showed her dozen chicks how to pick out the currants from this new delicacy. I swooped down on the brood and snatched it from them, for friends were still with us and we had nothing much for tea. I dusted it a little and felt it would pass, and wondering whether Evan Jones would have any recipe for replacing lost currants, I left the Buff Orpington making querulous noises, unable to believe her eyes as she scratched in the grass.

The prospect of getting the load safely up the stream bed was too much. I took from the rucksack everything in jars, bottles or tins and, leaving it all in the Canol stable-manger, put the wet loaf and the cake in the rucksack. No sooner had I started than the clutch wire came out of its soldered anchorage, and I was unable to change gear. Once more I dismounted and balanced the lever with the end of the wire pushed into it on a flat rock. I lifted the biggest stone I could find, and staggered with it, clutched to my bosom and dropped it on top of the lever. It jammed it together and worked long enough to get me in sight of the house before it broke again. I left the Eagle and walked home, noting with disapproval as I left, that my work with the heavy stone had broken two spokes and flattened the exhaust pipe a little more.

" One can have too much change of air," I said to Mat. " I shall have to go down again to-morrow to get the Eagle mended."

After breakfast I went out, shook the dew from its battered saddle, started down the valley with the clutch wire tied to my knee, lifting the clutch by the simple expedient of levering my left leg gently on to tiptoe, and making sudden erratic darts as I changed gear. A small cycle shop supplied a new wire, but after a brief inspection of the rock-battered lever, refused to have anything to do with the fitting of it, and I came back in the same fashion as I went, pondering on how to repair it with a stick of solder.

The gates that day reduced me to a kind of impotent savagery. None of them would open without my having to get off, for my tether allowed me no reach. To be tied to a motor cycle is very hampering. At every one came the irritating business of untying the wire, dismounting, finding a propping place for the Eagle while I set the gate ajar, retying the clutch wire, and giving the gate a fierce kick to get it open, to which it responded in its usual way by trying to do the same to me before I got through.

A message came up next day, passed on from mouth to mouth in that casual manner of country dwellers that is often quicker than sending a telegram, that a parcel awaited us at the station.

I went down. The station was quiet and empty. Behind

the ticket window the shutter was down, and the signal box had the air of one taking a siesta. Beneath the tollbridge little waves lapped at its feet, and small groups of waders stood motionless on the sandy spits running out into the estuary. Through the silence I could hear the dull thud of an axe being used somewhere in the woods above.

Among the labelled bicycles, sacks, boxes and packages of sheep-dip in the tiny waiting-room I found my parcel, looking wilted and ill at ease. The rope round it, taut when I sent it off, was slack and sagging, giving it the appearance of one who had suffered a long illness, and as I picked it up it bent limply over. The booking office came out of its coma so that I could sign for its safe arrival, for it certainly looked unable to vouch for it itself. I unroped it and carried the contents outside—an unassembled clothes horse, a pair of boots, a draining board, a bucket, and several tins of evaporated milk —these last being an emergency stock for the hot days when the milk turned sour.

At the curve by Evan Jones' house I was uneasily conscious that we were only missing his garage by an inch or two. Thinking of the bends ahead, I unstrung the bucket and tucked it behind Mrs. Evan Jones' garden wall, a useful temporary resting place for many things that I have felt indisposed to carry further.

A few minutes later I left the draining board behind a pile of hay in the chapel yard, and thus lightened, rode home. In the cool of the evening we walked down to retrieve the rest. They were, at any rate, all part of the way home.

But as this kind of thing went on, we resolved that as we couldn't make the journeys any easier by improving the Eagle, we'd attack the problem from another angle and improve the track instead.

A survey of the job forced us to modify this rather sweeping intention, and we decided, as a modest beginning, to start where our track diverted from the main track, and to continue in the homeward direction. To keep up the spirit of our first resolve, we wrote our fifth letter to the Council, pointing out that the public path, passing through our yard, was rapidly falling into disrepair, and would soon be entirely

PREPARATIONS FOR FRONT ROOF REPAIR WITH ACCLES AND POLLOCK SCALING LADDERS, THE STEPS AND THE FIVE RUNGERS

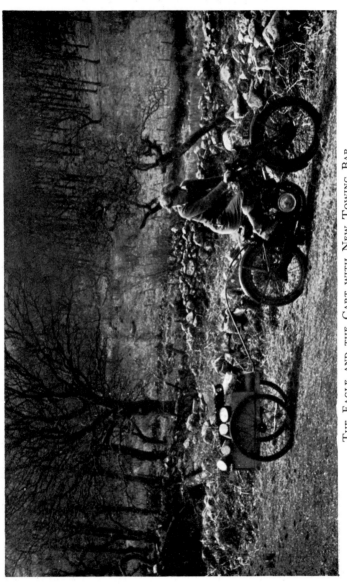

THE EAGLE AND THE CART WITH NEW TOWING BAR

obliterated unless they took it in hand. This was, I think, an understatement ; I have never been able to identify any of it except a section two miles beyond us in the next valley.

We started off to the repair work with pick, shovel, crowbar and buckets loaded into the cart, and began at the point furthest from home, the first deep pool on the rutty Canol track. We removed large sections of turf from its eastern shore and picked, hewed and shovelled until we had a deep gutter to drain off the water. When all was ready we opened the dam of turf, and the flood disappeared swiftly and smoothly, like bath water going down the drain. Looking over the wall, we saw it flowing to join the main stream. It was all very satisfactory. Into the muddy hole we threw big stones, medium-sized stones and little stones, and topped up the surface with all the gravel washed down the slate-quarry track in the cloudburst. If only we could have borrowed a steam roller for a couple of days, we could have pounded up and down that track and brought its surface up to the standard of an autobahn.

By tea time we had progressed slowly along to the Canol, levering out a rock here, filling up a hole there, and curious objects we had become, with arms, legs and faces mud-spattered from the splashes of the stones we had heaved into the smaller pools.

Before tea we bathed in the stream, and in struggling to improve the pool, improvements now being in our blood, we let slip a gigantic boulder that we were trying to shift so as to give us swimming room. It heeled slowly over, with a great splash and topple, and a few seconds later up floated a casualty—a fat trout, silver belly upwards, killed by the percussion.

For tea we had fried trout, increased from its original modest size by puffed-up batter, and set out again to start on the Canol paddock, a soft, turfy patch, which collects, in a depression yards long, the water draining from the Canol lane.

It was a lovely evening as we strolled down the fields. The sun was just leaving the bottom of the cwm, and lit the sides of the Garn with a deep warm glow as it crept higher towards the summit. The swallows darted through air so still that we could hear the bleating of the faint dots of sheep away at the top of the mountain. The rock clefts on the slopes were black and sharp, the dropping sun pierced far into the belt of oaks at the foot and illumined the dark, silent tangle of trunks within. Harebells in the grass were that brilliant blue they take on near the end of daylight, and Cader had the warm look she occasionally assumes when she intends, somewhere about sunset, to turn a glorious pink for twenty brief seconds.

The paddock was full of midges of a particularly vituperative kind as we removed the entire top spit of muddy turf, leaving it stacked in a neat compost heap against the wall. A lot of jigsaw work went into this section, for we relaid it entirely in crazy paving, carrying all the big, flat stones we could find in the paddock, fighting and wrestling with them to heave them from the stream, and rolling them from the fallen walls about the house.

At the top of the stream-bed track, we attempted to divert the spring that constantly directs a steady flow of water over the surface. We dug a ditch in the thick, oozy bog, hoping it would carry the water to the main stream. After much heavy work, bringing up unwilling spadesful of peat, we saw that our ditch was running uphill. A sizeable stream had collected in it, and was flowing happily along to help the spring in watering the track. We threw back all the sods and peat so laboriously dug and dammed it up again.

In the higher field were piles of small stones, collected at some time long past by the first tillers of the land, and walled round into little enclosures. So long had they lain that scrub oaks pushed through them. They were odd, bizarre shapes ; the branches, where the ends had been nibbled by sheep and cattle, constantly changed direction in an attempt to escape, giving them an air of uncertainty as to what kind of tree they were meant to be.

We took the spade and tried to wrest from the piles enough small stones to fill the cart, hoping that when they had been scattered on the track, the surface water might run along beneath them and leave a drier top. It was a futile kind of job ; a few little pebbles gathered on the spade at each push. There was much noise but little result, and when we shot them out on to the track there was little result there either ; at least not the kind we had hoped for ; the water simply rose and flowed over them too.

We retired, defeated.

" It is wishful thinking," said Mat sadly, as we threw the tools into the cart and started up the fields, " ever to imagine we can drain a mountain track. The mountain can do so much more in an hour to the whole valley than we can do to one miserable pool in an afternoon."

" Yes," I agreed. " Think of the cloudburst."

But before we gave up road engineering, one more possible improvement presented itself.

" This switchback," said Mat, as we stumbled over it on the way to the shed, "—sometime we might have enough petrol again to come by car. Let's try and level it so that there's a decent drive-in. I used to get tired of crying over spilt milk here," she added reminiscently.

We took off the crests and put them in the troughs, and with this our attempts to improve communications ended. At least we had struggled to the last ditch.

I ran the cart into the shed and put away the tools. Ewes and their lambs stepped towards us, sniffing, anxious for us to be gone so that they could settle down for the night in the dry bracken under the shed. The heron passed over on his way to the estuary, and as the last crimson flush lit the sky behind Diphwys, the north face of Cader turned a brilliant pink for a few moments. The whole valley caught the reflection ; the walls, the rocks, the trees, the grass, even the midges for a brief space were seen through rose-coloured spectacles. Sitting on the wall, we watched the colour change from red to grey like the glowing embers of a fire as they turn to ash. The clear air was already becoming chilly, and the smell of September was in it. Autumn was on its way. Shutting the door, we lit the lamp and blew up the fire ; the big iron kettle began to sing and shot its jet of steam to mix with the fragrant smell of wood-smoke eddying around the kitchen.

CHAPTER XII

NEW YEAR'S EVE of 1947, when the railways were nationalized, gave us the most comfortable train journey of our lives. Mat had the brilliant idea of travelling in a " Ladies Only." The crowd on that January night was small enough to allow us to *choose* a carriage. No ladies seemed to be travelling on the 12.5, and we sat bolt upright in the carriage of our choice at Paddington, with the lights on, looking out of the window with severe and forbidding expressions, such as we imagined ladies might wear. As midnight came, an engine somewhere gave a long melancholy toot, and the G.W.R. passed into the keeping of British Railways. We toasted its success in sherry drunk from the Thermos tops, and hoped its first act had been to throw open the refreshment room and light a fire in Ruabon waiting room for our arrival at dawn ; but it had slipped their memory, and Ruabon was exactly the same as usual.

When the train moved out, we were the only occupants of the carriage, and after a stunned silence, during which we took in our good fortune, we slept the whole night long, stretched out on the seats, waking only when the train stopped in the stations.

At Shrewsbury last night ended and to-day began. Sleepers awoke ; there was the clatter of cans and barrows, and the silence of the train was broken by the entrance of cheerful-looking men, freshly washed and shaved, with morning papers, dinner-tins, after-breakfast cigarettes and conversation.

At Penmaenpool the noise of the 12.5 died away to an almost inaudible mumble as it edged out and around the estuary. Seagulls were perched on the railings, their call sounding like the creaking of a rusty gate. The signalman looked out of his box with a New Year's greeting, and the tollbridge keeper made his usual smiling remark, " It's the long, long trail for you."

" I may be up to have tea with you one day this week," said the station master.

" You'll never walk as far as that. Look ! " said the tollbridge keeper, pointing to Diphwys. " All the way up there. Why, they won't get in themselves before to-morrow morning."

As we pulled the little cart past the chapel, Evan Jones was coming down with a flock of sheep.

" We are expecting you to supper this week," he said. " And your friends from Maestryfer and Cesailgwm Bach too."

There was a panting noise of machinery, and Willie's little green van appeared round the corner. Its radiator was still leaking water.

" The foxhunt is coming up the valley to-morrow," he told us. " You must come and," he added, with a cheerful grin," bring your air pistol. If you do but get one slug into the fox he will die of lead poisoning."

About eleven o'clock next morning, there gathered in our fields a couple of foxhounds, a few Nettles, several other dogs of no definite breed, and about six men, each with his lunch and a gun. We had a day of walking up one mountainside and down another at a speed rivalling the Lakeland fell walkers, and we saw a fox—but he saw us first !

Supper at Mrs. Evan Jones' was a wonderful pre-war kind of meal—the kind one had forgotten ever existed, and Iolo and Evan Jones had what appeared to be a delightful time in one corner for half an hour or so, making jokes either too abstruse or too simple for the rest of us, but judging from the effect on them—brilliant. When at last we all started up the lane homewards, we found a black impenetrable night and pouring rain and at the chapel we parted and took our divers ways. Up the track, we could feel our way by the walls, but when we reached the open spaces of Blaen-y-cwm fields, we had the rather frightening experience of being lost for an hour in our own bog. When we eventually got out of lit, we emerged at some point at right angles to the path, losing our bearings again, reaching home at last by the drunkard's expedient of clinging to the wall by the wood until it brought us to our own small gate.

The rest of the holiday—at any rate the after-dark part of it—went in long, leisured periods of reading ; and then it was over again, and we were down at the toll bridge on our way home.

" Until next time——" and the keeper raised his hand in salute.

That summer, we managed to save enough petrol to take us to Wales and back by road and in August we returned with great pleasure to planning a 1 a.m. start. Going over the possible calamities and their antidotes the evening before, Mat suddenly said, as she tucked the spare petrol can into the boot,

" You know, we ought to take a can of water with us, too."

" Why ? " I asked, mystified.

" The radiator leak," she replied. " If it happens again, we don't want to go hunting for water in the middle of a dark night."

The radiator, with increasing age, had developed a curious kind of leak ; for days it was apparently watertight, and then, without warning, it would leak away its entire contents in one quick gush. The last time this had happened we were in St. James' Park. I had drawn into the kerb as soon as I heard the pinking.

" Aren't our policemen wonderful ? " commented Mat. " Always there when you want them. Ask him where you can get water, and tell him not to suggest the lake—it's too far."

Acting on his suggestion, I went down the little path labelled " Ladies," to ask the attendant for a bucket of water. But there was no attendant, and what was more important—no bucket, and the only tap I could see, set in the wall, had no means of turning its squared end. I went back. The policeman was very busy. Could I reasonably trouble him further ? I felt not. Could he, anyhow, have provided me with a bucket ? Nearer to Buckingham Palace was one of those encampments left by road repairers, roped round, a hut in the middle, tools and debris around it. We walked down to it, and leaning over the rope, I picked up a battered bucket which Mat slung on one arm, and carried blatantly up the Mall as though it was a fashionable kind of shopping basket. We went down the path again and I tried to turn the tap with a spanner, but it was immovable. We thought again, and I returned to the car to prize off a hub cap. This, I thought, would solve it. There was only this way left, for the wash-basins, if any, seemed to be behind a locked door. We pooled our pennies and raised five, leaving the doors gently ajar. Each chain we pulled in turn, catching a hub capful of water in each, and tipping it into the bucket. By the time we had reached the fifth, the cistern of the first was full again, and when we had got the whole place sounding like a small Niagara, with five hissing cisterns and water splashed everywhere, the attendant returned.

" What—the—dickens ? " said she, slowly and ominously, and I can still remember the awful expression she had put into those three words. It was, when we came to settling up, an expensive bucketful. I agreed with Mat. We would take a can of water.

The main roads were quiet and empty at the start, approaching vehicles being heralded by their headlights from far away. As we travelled round the North Circular road with its curious variations in street lighting, one stretch in a golden glow, the next in ghastly blue, and a short section in a romantically rosy haze, the Singer was warmed up and purring nicely.

Mat, by the side of me, tried to sleep. Mat's trouble on a night journey is that she invariably wants to sleep when it is her turn to drive, and when she should be sleeping, for much of the time she is wide awake. If one tries to adjust matters, and magnanimously offers to change the programme and let her drive then and there, she immediately becomes sleepy, so that there is really nothing one can do.

I could always keep awake if I thought of Space. Where did Space end, and what did the end of Space look like ? Space must have an end, and yet, how could it ? Whatever came afterwards would need space to go into. The question became more and more enormous and involved, and at the end of fifteen minutes' thinking of Space, I was fully awake and immensely awed.

This year, Mat was working for her L.R.A.M., and had learnt pages and pages of questions and answers on music theory. I helped to keep her awake when it was her turn to drive, by asking her some of them. But it had odd effects on her driving.

" Define Sonata form," would give us a long period of easy, steady progress. " Volte Subito," and we would shoot suddenly forward. Questions like that I kept for the open road, and in the towns, small and with all their lights extinguished, I stuck to " Poco a poco," " Lento," " Andante."

Lorry traffic was thick for the first half of the night. From miles ahead they came, cresting the undulations in the distance, specks of sidelights and glare of foglights growing bigger and more dazzling, and then a great hulk loomed up, and like ships that pass in the night, they swept by and receded, smooth and Diesel engined ; something out of another life, leading a strange, nocturnal existence between city and city, eating up mile after mile in relentless progress. At Weedon, to our relief, they left us to go or come from the industrial purlieus of Coventry and Birmingham, and A5 was our own again, except for the sporadic headlights of other solitary travellers like ourselves.

When it was time for Mat to drive, she had managed to go to sleep, her head rolling about in a most dangerous-looking manner—as though it might snap off at any minute.

I woke her ; we changed places, and as soon as I was settled in the passenger's seat, I dozed at once. Dozing is almost nicer than sleeping ; one is just conscious of how pleasant it is, whereas sleeping is pure oblivion. I was aware, in the dim recesses of my mind, of our rather erratic progress. First we moved slowly, and then rattled along at a good pace. This cycle repeated itself for a long time. Eventually we came to a stop, and then started again—going backwards. I dozed on, bemusedly wondering why Mat found it better to drive backwards, but unwilling to pull myself together to find out. Then we stopped altogether and I slept. I woke up I don't know how long afterwards and found Mat was sleeping too. Daylight had almost come and we were in a small lane that I had never seen before. I woke her up.

" Too sleepy to go on," she muttered. " Eyes were rolling about." We wrapped our rugs tighter and slept again.

We had breakfast in a cornfield, with the spirit kettle simmering in the long dewy grass of the hedge-side, just as a summer dawn was turning to day. Rabbits were sitting up in the light mist a few yards away, a thrush sang from the big elm beside us, and an early mower cut his swathes at the other side of the field.

A few miles on, the throttle control broke. I stood on the running board with the bonnet up and worked the throttle by hand, while Mat changed gear and steered. Changing gear was a very complicated and delicately timed operation with two minds concerned in it. There was no refinement such as double de-clutching. I held on to the windscreen and when I felt safe enough, I shouted,

" Now ! " The gear shot in, and the car shot forward.

" Don't drive so jerkily," I bellowed reprovingly. " You'll have me off."

" I'm not driving," she shouted angrily back. " I'm steering. You're managing the speed."

The remark surprised me. It was impossible I felt. How could the driver be me on the running board and not Mat behind the wheel ? I reflected and realized it was true. Whether I was jerked off or not was in my own hands. We went, with reasonable smoothness to Shrewsbury, where we had a new wire fitted.

As we topped the pass from Dinas Mawddwy, I ceased to worry about all that can happen to old cars and the people who travel in them, and projected my mind ahead to contemplate all the things that can happen to an old house, through a long absence, without people.

The first relief was to get over the pass, for from there one could roll down to Dolgelley even if the engine had fallen out, and from Dolgelley, we could, as a last resort, push the car to the bottom of the valley. Having got so far, there were such things as the kindliness of Evan Jones with his tractor. There were home-made carts. In the uttermost extremity, there were feet and rucksacks.

The gates up the hill had grown more dilapidated, and the post of the first one shook in its socket like a loose tooth. The one beyond Willie's which had a habit, when it tired, of peevishly throwing on the ground the iron eyes from which its hinges depended had collapsed entirely, and lay propped up. Timber hauliers had left on the slopes below it a devastation of lopped trunks and fallen branches ; deep tractor ruts ran through the rough grass, and the surface of the track was ploughed into furrows where the loads had been carted.

The position of the bog gate at the top of the stream bed told us the summer had officially come to the valley. The gate there is a kind of symbol of a movable feast, for when autumn comes and the grass of the little fields grows brown and withered, it is removed and left propped by the wall, leaving the sheep and bullocks free to wander and find sustenance where they can. When the grass begins to push through green and fresh again, it is put back, and the animals find nurture again in a smaller and more confined space. In the smooth field beyond it, chaffinches, and yellow-hammers brighter than canaries, flitted from one group of scrub-oaks to the next.

We drove into the shed over the improved humps, and swung the kitbag over the wall, groping at the bottom of it for the keys put safely there at the end of the last holiday, and still there with all the clean laundry on top. After a few groping moments of doubt, up they came ; the *key*-keys, so to speak, which opened the first essential doors. Battering ram tactics on the swollen door burst it suddenly open, knocking a still deeper dent in the hall plaster where the Yale knob struck.

The hall seat was veiled in cobwebs, dead spiders, woodlice rolled in little balls like hedgehogs, bits of bracken and sheeps' wool, and the peacock butterflies that had clung to the beams since last summer, to flutter down, dead, or half dead, with every draught from the open door.

Some kind of bush telegraph summoned up the current herd of bullocks, and they stood waiting, ready as usual, if vigilance relaxed, to eat brown paper, string or kit bags.

We had an elaborate system of keys : the major ones we took home with us, the minor keys stayed behind, locked up by the major ones. Each door key has a white oblong label, those for cupboards, drawers or chests bear a circular one in red, green or yellow, according to which part of the house they belong. Coloured labels made the preliminary sorting so much easier in a dim wintry light ; and on summer days, too, when the valley below has disappeared, and the house floats alone and disembodied in a sea of mist, peering for a coloured label was easier than trying to decipher the written name on key tags in the thin grey light. When each key, with its dangling and colourful label was in place, the effect was, as Kath remarked, of a house in which the money-conscious owners have left the price tag on all articles.

The first half hour was always depressing, for so much seemed to have happened to the house since we left it. It depended largely on what weather the valley had endured in our absence, and as we walked from room to room noting the amount of fallen plaster, mice depredations, new fungus or patches of green moss, we had ten minutes or so of dark depression ; a kind of mental catharsis we allowed ourselves as we sat on the bottom of the stairs and moaned at what a term's wet weather can do to a house left dry and tidy.

We settled down to the remedies ; first the fire—the quickest step to a change of spirit and looks, both in the animate and inanimate occupants. I took from the cupboard a mice-nibbled newspaper, sodden like all else, an armful of twigs and some coal. Coal was the one thing that never seemed to get damp ; we were grateful for this one mercy. I fetched a dram of paraffin, and scraping out the wet clogged wood-ash of our last fire, relaid and lit it. For the first few minutes, it was very uncertain as to whether it meant to burn at all : the flame wavered and died down, flared up again where it met a spot of paraffin, died down again and went out entirely when it could no longer fight against wet newspaper and damp twigs. It needed several

attempts, but once it had shown willing, I gave it no chance
to change its mind. With the bellows, I blew on it hard :
first came a thin wheezy noise as the flame flickered un-
certainly, and as it took hold, a deep roar as of a fire raging
through a forest, as the flames were drawn back into the
bellows spout, to roar out in hot air at the next blow.

Within half an hour, there was a great blaze leaping up
the chimney, lighting the damp walls in sudden revealing
flickers, and brightening the surface of the furniture. As I
looked round, I felt a surge of pleasure at the sight of it :
there is something peculiarly one's own about furniture one
has bought as unplaned boards, transported, sawn, planed,
chiselled, fitted and polished to a piece of furniture which,
although it has not quite come up to the first conception, at
least bears a strong resemblance. to it.

Mat filled the iron kettle at the trough until we had time
to deal with the blocked tap, and swung it from the hook
and chain dangling from the chimney. As it began to sing,
my heart lifted too : there could not be much wrong with a
house that had a blazing fire and a singing kettle. We
swept the kitchen floor, wiped the mildew from furniture
which stood in the darker corners, and blackleaded the rusty
grate. Upstairs, I pulled open the door of the wardrobe,
and prepared to receive the roped and rolled carpet, pushed
protestingly in, weeks ago, and ready to fall out into my
waiting arms as soon as the chance came.

To lay the carpet was the second step to making the kitchen
the cheerful place we remembered. When the hearthrugs
were down, the coloured crockery on the dresser, and the
books taken from the drawers and put on their shelves the
kitchen took on its friendly air, and the chill, musty atmosphere
of arrival evaporated ; a log or two on the fire, and the
crude, pungent smell of coal smoke was superseded by the
lovely and delicate smell of blazing oak or birch.

We took the bedding and hurled it through the open bedroom window. It was quicker than carrying it down. There
we spread it out to dry on the walls and the clothes rope. I
chased the cattle far enough and furiously enough for them
to feel that there would be no welcome if they returned.

Wet days were a different matter ; we then got out the outsize clothes horse (called in my young days, by the much prettier name of " Winter's hedge "), and on it draped the blankets to air before the fire. The first time we did this, the density of the apparently never-ending clouds of steam had appalled us, and on returning home we took a blanket from a bed there, and held it in front of the fire. It was meant as a sort of test case : if it didn't steam, we must do something about the condition of our Welsh beds. If it steamed, then our Welsh beds were no worse than our English ones. To our relief, it steamed, though not with quite the same thick volumes of vapour as the Welsh blankets.

After that, we ceased to bother about damp blankets any more : sometimes we aired them, sometimes they went straight on the beds—it all depended on how tiring the journey had been. Once, we went further and slept in them wet. We were having tea, with eyes slowly closing in anticipation of bed. I think mine were already shut, and I was eating, not by sight, but by instinct, when Mat leapt to her feet. " It's raining," she said, and dashed out of the door.

It took me a few seconds to bring myself back to this world, and to wonder why rain at this particular moment was of such importance when we had endured days of solid rain, and then I remembered—the whole of our bedding lay out there in a thunder-shower that was already over. We brought it in, looked at it, felt it and shook it, but beyond that, we just could not bring ourselves to do anything more about it. The 12.5 had been too tiring, the little cart too heavy ; the fire had taken too long to fan into a blaze. All that mattered was sleep, and a place to rest our weary bodies. We made our beds, and we lay on them, and apart from a damp clamminess that I was conscious of in a dim sort of way throughout the night, it was not too uncomfortable.

Perhaps, as we have been told, we shall suffer for our rashness with rheumatism in old age. Perhaps we shall, if we ever reach old age in this uncertain world. Maybe, if we do, there will be, by that time, a cure for rheumatism. One weighs up the pros and cons and chooses. We chose unaired blankets, and beds at six o'clock. We air bedding only for friends.

The mattresses were too big to throw through the window, and these we carried downstairs. They were awkward things to take up and down stairs : I found they always tended to struggle. Half way down, it was often better to let go, for they seemed to prefer to arrive at the bottom by themselves.

Meanwhile, in the dairy, the bread-pan and table tops were being scrubbed, plaster swept up and food put away. I filled up the Primuses, and in the kitchen oven crammed twigs to dry for next day's fire.

New packets of envelopes were unpacked, and wrapped quickly in cellophane, before the damp air stuck their flaps firmly down. Through the years, we have amassed in that house enough envelopes with firmly stuck flaps to stock a small stationer's shop.

The Dulcitone, a late acquisition and one of our indoor joys, was given to us by friends who had stayed with us. We brought it downstairs and set it on its spindly legs near the fire to dry out its damp keys, and looked out the few volumes of Purcell, Bach and Arne kept on the bookshelves for it.

There were mousetraps to set—mousetraps that went off almost as soon as one's back was turned. So unsophisticated are our mice that we once caught two in the same trap at one setting. On the second day they were more wary, and on the third day, having taught them that it was dangerous to pick up food in a house, we declared a truce, and so long as they did not push themselves on our notice, it was live and let live.

From the medicine chest we threw out the disintegrating aspirins and cascara tablets with their dark brown insides bursting through their skins with the damp. The barometer was hung and tapped. " More wind," it had read when we left. " More wind," it read when we returned. Some day, if that barometer is correct, a veritable tornado, Beaufort scale twelve, will sweep the valley. I set the needle and wound the downstairs clock, and the machinery of the house now being geared up, we went to bed.

We set the alarm, a long and intricate process made necessary by the antiquity of our alarm clock, for it never goes off at the time promised. It might have to be set at three to ring at eight, and something seems to happen to it every time we go away, for next time it may have to be set at eight to ring at three.

" Now ! " said Mat, " concentrate, and see that we are doing this properly. Clock hands to the time we want to get up . . ."

" Nine," I said, " then wind everything and turn the alarm pointer——"

" —until the bell rings. What comes next ? " she asked.

" Switch off the bell, leave the alarm pointer where it is, and turn the face hands back to the proper time again."

" I hope the end of summer-time doesn't come while we are here. Remember how we went through three days two hours ahead of everybody else, through your silly argument ? "

" Yes," I said apologetically. My argument was that if dark was to fall earlier we must put the clock hands forward to accommodate it, but somehow the system never accommodated us, and at changes to and from summer-time our times were always out of joint.

We put the alarm clock on the table. It was not so much that we wanted to get up early, but that we wanted to be sure of staying in bed long enough, for one early holiday, we woke, and seeing daylight through the window, assumed that morning was already upon us. Rather unwillingly, we got up and set about breakfast and fire-making. The red embers gave no clue, and it was only when breakfast was over and dark came that we realized it had been supper, and groped happily back to bed again.

Sometimes I still woke on summer evenings of the days of arrival, and went fishing in the nearer pools, and for long it was possible to persuade Mat that she had slept all night and all day, and it was now the night after the night she had gone to bed. It was only when she started to put a foot out of bed that I relented.

Satisfied that we should not unwittingly make the horrible mistake of getting up on the wrong day, we went to sleep, and my last impression was of air blowing through the open windows, flinging back the curtains, tinkling the key labels as it blew in, strong and clean and pushing out the damp and ancient smell. In its place came the smell of wet earth and bracken, and the last sound before I swam into sleep was a baa in the garden below and an answering baa from the fields, and the sound of the stream as it gurgled through the tangle of rushes on its way to the bog.

I woke to the sound of a wren perched on the small gate ; its volume of song was as loud and clear as that of the missel thrushes which stormed from the chimney tops in winter.

Hopes had been growing since last autumn, and I was living again in a phantasy-world where four pounders dashed for the overhang in the pool.

Before I went to look for them I thought it would be as well to know whether we had a bull. It was useful to know at least his nominal whereabouts.

Willie's brother Dick was over with the sheep in the small cwm, and I walked across to ask him.

" What about last year's bull ? Is he up here ? "

" My father sold him to a man near Towyn ; he was a very savage animal, and nearly killed someone."

" Thank goodness he is out of our cwm then," I thought callously, and went back with great satisfaction to get my tackle ready and to tell Mat that we were bull-free for the holiday.

I went downstream to the big pool where I have never yet caught anything. Each year hope springs afresh as I think of the fat trout which must lurk beneath those still weeds, and each year I return empty handed. I expect this will go on all my life. At any rate, expectation gives zest. I settled down to drop the worm quietly in, and let it float gently under the willows ; and as it was carried slowly along in the current I leaned against a boulder and looked up at the cloud shadows moving across Mynydd Mynach. I could hear a woodpecker in the Canol damsons, and magpies were flying across to the wood. I thought of Dick's summing-up of their depredations as I watched them.

" They are very good bad birds," meaning that they are bad birds of the very first order.

" But they are very lovely birds," I thought as I dropped my worm in again.

Suddenly, in the peace, there was a crashing noise in the hedge of the opposite bank, and a blackthorn bush was parted neatly down its middle. I watched, startled. The parting widened, and there came into sight an ugly black head, with the short white horns that had become very familiar.

" A very big bullock," I thought. " Big enough for a bull. If I didn't know he was elsewhere, I could easily imagine he *was* a bull."

But I took no chances. Groping behind me for the wall, I slowly withdrew backwards, like one making an obsequious departure from Royalty. Then the complete head came through and I saw the short, stocky forequarters there was no mistaking. I ran, and fear lent me wings. I wondered as I ran whether bulls can swim. I hoped not : but I hoped, too, that he would try, for the pool was deep enough to drown him, and that would be the end of him.

What he did I made no attempt to discover ; the important thing was that I heard no heavy galloping behind me.

" Willie," I said to him that evening as he poured our milk into the can, " what is that big creature on the other side of the pool ? "

" Why, he is the bull."

" But I thought he had gone to Towyn."

" Ah, but this is the new one. He is a fine, big animal."

Big he certainly was : as to the fineness I do not know. It is not judged by any ordinary criterion. I left the fishing of the big pool and we took to the safer occupation of bilberrying.

Bilberries of an immense size grew on the terraced slopes of the mountains. Iolo swears he has gathered them the size of cherries, but this may be a fisherman's story, for the largest I ever found, after much assiduous searching, never exceeded sloe size.

There was never any doubt as to when the bilberry season opened. Iolo we looked upon as our official opener, and from the gap in the wall of the lake track he gave a wild yell towards Blaen-y-cwm on the way up, an indication that in a couple of hours or so they would be with us for tea. On the return there was a wilder yell as they climbed the wall, a warning that it was time to put the kettle on, and we sit on the wall in the sun and wait, watching for the first glimpse of them slithering down the wood. If we were not occupied in bolstering up the house, we, too, went up to join them at the first yell.

The yell that holiday came on the third day, and from the miscellaneous collection of garments in the wardrobe we selected the oldest trousers, seats stained purple from past bilberry pickings. Picking is an occupation when it is every man for himself. If you need cigarettes you must carry them with you, for after the first ten minutes you see no more of your friends until you join them for the walk back. The easiest method of gathering is to wear an empty syrup tin tied round one's neck. It must have a lid: and when one has endured the agony of seeing the afternoon's harvest pour hopelessly away among the deep heather stems and rocks, one learns early to put the lid on when moving from ledge to ledge.

Booted, trousered and pocketed, we started up the wood. I slung the binoculars on, too ; they saved much scrambling : I could see whether it was worth climbing a fierce-looking slab in the hope of finding cherry size, or whether they would be of currant dimensions when I got there. Up on the lake track, with a sense of being high above the world, we ambled towards the bilberry slopes with the pleasant sound of our boot-nails ringing on rock.

As we crossed over to the mountain slopes, sheep lying in the shelter of rock or heather sprang up and bounded off as though they had seen the devil himself. Up here, the sheep were wild and ran madly at the first sight of a human being, though frequently, when they were over their first fright, they turned and advanced a few angry steps, stamping their feet. These mountain sheep had a call of their own which we never heard among the more domesticated ones below. It was a sharp whistling sound, like a rather breathy sneeze, and for long I thought it was the call of some strange bird, which always seemed to keep aggravatingly out of sight.

Kath and Iolo were already over the first foothill, and we stumbled through the deep heather in search of a prolific ledge. There was a timelessness about those afternoons which I felt in few other occupations. Up there, alone in a sea of bilberries, the blue lake far below, the wide, clear sky above, the bold and wonderful sweep and stab of mountains on every horizon, one felt utterly remote from the world below. Companions scattered and were soon out of sight and earshot ; the only sounds were the call of wheatear and pipit, the dry rustle of the breeze through whin and heather, a far-away bleat of a sheep, or the sudden buzz of a bee as it passed, and as sudden a silence as it disappeared. Everything was so calm and unhurried. For the whole afternoon, one saw no movements bigger than a bird's flight, or a sheep grazing its way foot by foot along the lake's edge, reduced to inch by inch through distance. There was a prevailing sense of peace, a tremendous feeling of space and silence and sunlight as the hours wheeled by, until a sinking sun and cooler air reminded me that Time cannot be suspended for more than a short span. The descent to the track felt like a return to a world that had stopped whilst one had clambered high up there in the shadows and sun and stillness.

Often I have been startled, the feeling of solitariness heavy upon me on the sides of that great cwm, to sense rather than see, a tiny figure making its way to the foot. Solitude, I think, gives one a heightened receptiveness to small changes : one is aware at once of slight alterations in sounds and movements, however vast the place.

It was always difficult knowing when to foregather again. Shouting was of little use. It might carry a mile in one direction and not more than a few yards in another. I have shouted myself hoarse and heard the echo carry back from the Garn, with no answering shout, yet I knew that I could not be more than two hundred yards from the others.

The only way was to set a time limit, and perversely the biggest bilberries appear when it is time to go. They can never be found next day either ; it is almost impossible to locate the exact place one saw them, as though the mountain resented too familiar a knowledge of itself and prevented a return.

Down on the track Iolo was rushing about in the long heather.

" Where is it? Where's it gone ? " he lamented. " I've lost it ! "

" Lost what ? " I inquired.

" My big brown-paper parcel," he said, poking into another clump. " Ah ! here it is," and he clutched it triumphantly to his heart.

" But what is it ? " I asked him.

" A present from Diphwys," he said mysteriously.

We started back down the track to tea, the low sun casting our immensely long shadows with ridiculously long legs ahead of us.

As we tumbled over the fence into the bog he tore off the brown-paper wrappings and disclosed a large hot-water jug.

" For you," he said benevolently—" to put hot water in," he added as an afterthought.

" But won't you need it yourselves ? " inquired Mat politely.

I had already seized it in gratitude, not having considered or cared whether he needed it or not.

" Oh, no ! " said he decisively ; " we never drink hot water."

CHAPTER XIII

NEXT day we started earlier and went farther afield to see whether bilberries grew on the Rhinogs. They were currant size and grew sparsely, and we left them and climbed instead to the gap of the Rhinogs. Sheltered by the wall, we sat looking down to the black depths of Llyn-y-Bi, while the wind tore boisterously up from the Irish Sea across the slaty sides of the dark and evil-looking Llyn Hywel on the seaward side of the pass. Far away in the distance the sun shone on blue water and yellow sand. Cloud shadows swam majestically over the land and wild-looking sheep scattered at our approach. On a very far ridge, the wild goats were disappearing over a crest.

As we neared home, some hours later, the last few steps down the steep wood brought that lovely sense of aching limbs and acute pleasure in anticipation of bed. After days like that, we ignored milk and post. Pulling off our boots, leaving them scattered about the hall, we staggered upstairs, stiff-limbed, shedding garments as we went.

" Sleep after toil, port after stormy seas——" There was never any interval between pulling up the bedclothes and sleep. The quickest way of getting to sleep is not to count imaginary sheep jumping through imaginary gaps. It is to go out on the summits for a day and watch real ones—especially the high ones—the whistlers.

Towards the end of the week we took the Singer down to meet Toni at the station. Evan Jones was by the bottom bridge.

" My potatoes are ready," he said cheerfully. " There is a fork in the row that I am digging. Good carrots and big lettuces, too. You must go up and get some. Better far than those in the shops."

We climbed the gate to the field where we had dug potatoes last year, forgetting that there was such a thing as rotation of crops, or the three-field system. There were no potatoes there. It was a sweltering day, and we went slowly down the hill again and climbed back to the track, leaving it to try the next field. Still no potatoes. We returned to the first field and through the gate to the one above it. There were none there either. I began to wonder whether there was a special dwarf Alpine species of potato, suitable for high altitudes, and hard to find in the long grass. We toured the whole of Evan Jones' land before finding in the highest and farthest corner of it several rows of normal-sized potatoes. The pleasures of digging them, new and straw-coloured from the clean, wet-smelling earth, was lost on me that afternoon.

That hot, moist summer, for the first time in our experience, our fields grew mushrooms. They gave me great pleasure, for I love not only eating but picking mushrooms—the little white satiny buttons, with the tiny frill just breaking round the gills, and the clean way they come up, leaving a small hole in the earth. My promised land would have not milk and honey, but mushrooms and gooseberry pie.

The bullock field was dotted with mushrooms, and we gathered them morning and evening : far too many for us to use, but dispensing them like the Ladies Bountiful to others whose fields grew none.

The best of them grew in the corners of the field, and we fanned out to find them. Toni, hidden from us by a pile of stones, had found a prolific patch. Suddenly there was a falsetto bellow, and I looked up to see the bull calf charging with lowered head towards her as she came in sight again. Rather superfluously we shouted towards her :

" The bull ! " and rushed in her direction, picking up stones as we ran. As we had passed him earlier, we had given him the usual few kindly words. He had been an ordinary little bull calf, but now he seemed inflated to twice his size : and his head was changed from its podgy roundness to a determined squareness. His charge was over almost before it began. He went on until he was within a yard or two, and then gave a foolish sort of jump in the air, changing his direction as though to indicate that it had all been a dreadful mistake on his part, and skidded to a stop with his tail straight out behind him. He was a bull calf again. But it was sufficient warning. We avoided the mushroom fields until he was elsewhere.

We used to take a fearful kind of interest in the bull calves, attempting to ingratiate ourselves, scratching their heads when they lay in the shade of the house, and hoping they would remember our kindness when they grew up. They may have done, but whether they grew into our bulls, or were sold to ramp in other fields, with other owners benefiting from our early treatment of them, I do not know.

The hot weather continued and we went to Barmouth for a bathe.

As we drove round the corner of the Canol track we saw a pig swaggering along, grunting happily to himself as he nosed every object in his path. He was a ridiculous sight : a dirty pinkish pig, walking alone in the mountains on a summer afternoon, with his curly tail trembling in an ecstatic " Q ". Sitting down, we awaited his approach ; with bulls we had some sort of system, but for pigs we had, as yet, no formula.

We felt we ought to persuade him to return, but to shoo him all the way to Willie's with the car would have been an afternoon's job ; pigs are notoriously obstinate creatures.

" Let's put him in the back seat with Toni."

This conjured up a wonderful picture. If only I'd had my Leica with me, I would have made an attempt to get him there for the sake of the photograph.

" And send it to *The Tatler*," said Mat. " Miss Toni Booth and a friend start out for a bathe on the Welsh coast."

" He certainly needs one," I thought, seeing his grime-coated back as he came nearer.

He stopped with an inquiring grunt a few yards from the car and stared at us. We stared back : obviously something had to be done about him, for with that determined swagger he could reach Trawsfynydd, and his sides of bacon be lost for ever.

"Let's shut him in the Canol garden," I suggested, "and tell Willie where he is."

We knocked on the Canol door, thinking that perhaps they might have better suggestions to offer us.

" Here's the Isaf pig ; what shall we do with him ? "

They might have taken him in, but, as Mat hinted, they might slay and keep him. It was enough temptation. But there was no answer to our knock, and it seemed the garden was the best solution. I crept behind him, Toni and Mat, with flanking movements, placed themselves on either side. He blinked his small eyes suspiciously and gave a grunt, quivering his whole fat body. As it dawned on him that plans were afoot to destroy his afternoon and curb his late-found freedom, he took sudden, energetic action. With a series of bounds and squeals he was away around the corner to the paddock, where he stopped dead and peered back at us from under his floppy ears. But it was three to one : we got him on the move again and herded him, indignant and protesting, back up the Canol lane, and as we pushed his fat body by hand through the gateway into the garden, he gave a final high, outraged squeal, and settled down to plough up the earth with his unringed snout.

When we returned from the sea he was back in his sty ; his days were numbered.

" At Christmas," said Willie, " he will be dead."

" Is he ill, then ? " queried Mat.

" I mean he will be dead because we shall have killed him."

The holiday neared its end, Toni went back, and we spent the rest of the day packing the car for our own return. As we left the barn we noticed the ewe : a forward sort of ewe, who had got herself, by means which only she knew, into the field reserved for those proud and insolent creatures, the rams. Here they awaited the great moment when they would be turned loose on the mountain in November to find a harem. Dusk was falling when we noticed the rather untoward doings in this aristocratic enclosure. The rams were in a dense pack, and in the middle of the scrum was the ewe. It didn't seem to be quite what she had expected. They hounded the poor creature all round the field, and by the time they surged towards the gate she was exhausted, mouth open, head down and panting. We understood nothing of the intricacies of sheep breeding, but it seemed plain that this kind of thing should not be happening. Knowing nought of the eugenic grounds, we decided 'we must get her out on ethical ones.

We fetched the hurricane lamp, a rope, and a couple of fence posts for our own defence, climbed the gate, and, to the despair of the ewe, joined in the chase. Three times round that field we hared after the nimble-footed pack, until we, too, were in the same breathless state as the creature we proposed to rescue. The rams eyed us with their haughty and malevolent stare, stamping their feet like Spanish ballet dancers. We were near giving up when, by luck, we got them all cornered by means of the rope, their amber eyes gleaming in the light of the lamp, and one or two of the bigger ones advanced towards us threateningly. I gripped my fence-post tightly ; it would have given me great satisfaction to bring it down on one of those heads, but we needed all our attention for the rope and the lamp as we closed in on them. In a quick, concerted dash we fell upon the ewe. She was too weary to care or struggle, but the rams were not. There was a brief free-for-all as they jostled us in their attempts to regain her, but we bore her from the field victorious, and lifted the smelly, oily bundle to safety between the gate rails. For a short time she remained wedged and immovable, and I wielded my fence-post happily while Mat pushed her through. She fell with a soft thud into the green lane where sheep may safely graze, and I only hope she learnt sense from the experience.

There was no time to find out, for we were off soon after dawn next day, but doubtless emotional relationships were settled in the next month or two, and at Christmas, as we drove through our familiar fields again, rams and ewes were grazing peaceably together.

As we neared Isaf that Christmas evening to fetch the milk, Willie was driving out, a sense of urgency about the green van.

" He is dead ! " he shouted. " I am going to borrow a mincer. Will you come and help me cut him up ? Have you a long knife ? " he added as an afterthought, " or a saw ? "

" I hate the idea," said Mat to me. " It's like carving up a deceased acquaintance."

" But pork," I began persuasively, " pork—a thing you've not had since war began or ended. Pork—with crackling ! "

" It's not our pork," said Mat obstinately, " and it would be too tantalizing a thing to cut up someone *else*'s pork."

" There may be perquisites," I suggested.

" There may," she said.

I sensed a slight change of mind, which had hardened by breakfast time, and at six o'clock that evening we went down dressed in gas capes worn back to front to cope with what we felt might be a greasy and slippery job. The moonlight shone brilliantly into the empty sty.

" Where's my tenon saw ? " I asked, groping about on the Isaf settle. " Give me that long knife," muttered Mat. " ' Be bloody, bold and resolute.' I feel only one of them."

Armed, we descended to the cellar, lit by Willie's small son, who stepped carefully down the steep stairs, holding a stump of guttering candle. The smell down there was cold and dank. In a shadowed corner we saw him, hanging head downwards from the door lintel, a clean, pink corpse, suspended from a wooden bar. I could sense Mat's shudder as she braced herself for the ordeal.

" First we cut off his head," said Willie, and proceeded to do so. I didn't mind him so much with his head off ; he was no longer identifiable as a personality I had once known.

" Perhaps you will carry it upstairs," said Willie, teasingly, to Mat. She took what was held out to her with a shudder and her eyes shut, and stumbled towards the steps with the grinning head clutched to her bosom.

" You put an apple in his mouth before you leave him," I said as she put her foot on the first step.

" Now," said Willie to me, " you must hold him steady. I am going to cut him in two."

When he was almost in halves he slipped from my grasp and went down with a thud that shook the floor and knocked out the candle. Groping about, we found and re-lit it, and as I looked at the shadow of Willie and the long knife on the whitewashed wall, the corpse on the floor, the small wide-eyed child holding the candle high above his head, and Mat, in an oilskin buttoned down the back, I thought what an odd scene it all was.

"Back we must get him," said Willie, and somehow or other back we did get him on to his wooden support, and washed him clean with icy water before continuing with the job, and we carried the sides, cold and clammy, heavy and slippery, and laid them on the slabs upstairs. With what Tom Sawyer would have described as a " Genuine Barlow," a small clasp knife that a Wolf Cub might own as his first weapon, Willie dissected him with :

" For brawn.   For black puddings.   For frying.   For pies," and finally, " This we shall cure for bacon and ham."

We bore home with us a succulent piece of pork—" Perks," I whispered to Mat—and a parcel of slices for frying.   Ever since we have taken more than a cursory interest in the current pig, looking over his sty as we pass, noting his healthy or pallid look, and conjecturing on his dead weight in scores. Several Christmases his time has come while we have been at Blaen-y-cwm, and the request has come : " Will you bring your long knife and help to cut up the pig ? "

Later that week we were pulling up a load of lime in the cart.   At the top of the stream bed Mat said thoughtfully, " A boxful of lime would fit very easily on the back seat of the Singer."

" No," I said firmly.

" Well, then, fetch the motor cycle," she suggested.

Now this did seem a good idea.   I walked up for a rope and the Eagle ; and the Eagle, willing to have a little scamper before bedtime, bore me willingly down the fields.   We yoked her to the cart with the rope, and I tied the other end round my waist.   Mat exerted all her strength to keep the handle down so that the load stayed in the cart instead of sliding out of the back.   Apart from my being tugged almost over the back mudguard it worked, though Mat, running to keep up, was too breathless to give verbal approbation.   She merely nodded her head vigorously, and smiled with the pride of the inventor.

The idea seemed to be worth working out.   We must have

a towing bar.   I drew a sketch and took it to the blacksmith, spending a pleasant afternoon poking about in his dusty, cobwebbed smithy, and finding lovely bits of wrought iron, while he blew the bellows and heated and hammered the metal to the right shape.   From time to time we took it out and tried it on the Eagle like a new suit.   I fastened it to the frame and rode home, striking occasional sparks as the end hit against the rocky road.

Halfway up the valley was Evan Jones, a coat and spade slung over his shoulder.   I stopped to pass the time of day. His three gentle-eyed and gentle-mannered dogs trotted up and sat down, watching us, and sweeping the dusty earth with their tails.   Evan Jones is always very encouraging about new ideas.

" It is a useful thing indeed, that little cart of yours.   I would like one like that myself.   To take meal to the cattle it would be very useful.   And the handle now—you will be able to take me in the little cart to the Eisteddfod next year. I will remind you when the time comes."

We tied the handle more securely, and I started up the hill. I had left the fastenings off as I went down, so that I could joust at the gates with the front wheel.   The energy with which I banged them open had a reciprocal effect on the speed with which they banged shut, and when I was not swift enough in the retreat, they crashed viciously on to the back number plate and held me captive.

We took the participants into the first field for their maiden voyage.   To induce the cart to keep its distance, and not embarrass me by trying to overtake, I had the swivel joint made as far away as possible—at the cart end of the handle. I screwed it all up tightly and invited Mat to sit in the cart, while I rode gently round the field.   She was a trifle unwilling, but as I pointed out, all good causes have their martyrs.

Cautiously we rolled off.   After the first few seconds I wondered, since we were proceeding satisfactorily as a complete unit, whether I could safely change into top gear, when suddenly I felt as though I and the Eagle were being shaken from side to side by some force, lion-like in its strength.   I looked quickly round at Mat. She was affected too. She crouched in the cart, holding grimly to its sides as it leapt laterally from one wheel to the other. It seemed unable to travel on both wheels at the same moment. I stopped and she scrambled out very quickly.

I decided the cart probably needed ballast. We must find its plimsoll line. We lifted two large stones from the wall top and put them in. I had a much harder time persuading Mat to try it again. It was only when I had described in glowing terms how we could bring logs in loads once we got the hang of it, that she consented, and then only if I promised to stop at the first shout.

We moved off, and the first shout came almost at once. I felt the same terrific, earth-shaking movement, and looked round quickly to see the cart following me in the same erratic manner, on alternate wheels. Mat, with circular eyes and set jaw, was fending off the ballast as it crashed from one side of the cart to the other. For the time being that was the end of a very promising idea.

Since then Mat's brother has put his mind to work on it, and made it fit to take Evan Jones to the Eisteddfod. But the swivel joint is at the other end. It is the triumphant culmination of all experiments in transport—sled, cart, cycle, motor cycle to motor cycle and trailer.

Packing up day came all too soon. We put up the network of ropes from the upstairs beams, for the rugs to hang on and keep them safe from mice, for those mice are only a trifle less destructive than termites. Getting the rugs up was always a little like pancake-tossing ; we flung them hopefully up, and clean over the line they went, to fall upside down on the floor.

The tools were greased, boots and shoes laid out on the wall and oiled with veterinary castor oil, cement put in the best bedroom, and the Dulcitone borne upstairs, looking like a little coffin in its wrapping of cotton duck.

Cushions and spare pillows we pummelled into the cup-board, the kitchen was cleared, and by evening we were sitting in a stone-floored kitchen, with a minimum of crockery, one small lamp, and one chosen book each. Everything that could be packed away was packed, even the cushions of the easy chairs were slung from the bacon hooks, and we sat and read on the webbinged frames.

We set the alarm clock by the usual trial and error method, which becomes more of a trial and more frequently in error as the clock grows older. Its insistent buzz next morning struck a chill into my soul, for I could hear the rain battering in gusts on the window, and when the candle was lit could see the huge glistening drops on the dark panes.

To have a wet morning for departure is the worst thing that can happen. Packing a car in such weather is bad enough, for a few journeys between house and car are enough to soak one to the skin, but when, in addition, the chains have to be put on before the car will even move, it is the last straw. Wind and rain are such implacable enemies ; they never let up ; they give no quarter, but just relentlessly batter away, making the job four times harder. A wet morning when one goes by train is unspeakable ! We arrive at Penmaenpool utterly sodden, and stay so until evening.

My heart sank as I opened the door to the pitch-black morning, with wind and rain beating hard up the valley. We put on the chains, kneeling in mud, our heads in the exact line of the steady streams of water pouring off the corrugated roof. The jack canted slowly sideways just as the chains were nearly on, and to free it meant lying down in the morass of mud.

The maker's instructions on fitting chains struck me as particularly ironic on that morning. They sounded so delightfully simple. " There is no need to jack up the car. Simply lay the chains in a straight line behind the rear wheels and reverse the car on to them." It was precisely because the car would not reverse at all that we were putting on the chains.

When it was done we got into dry garments and on with the rest of the packing up.

My blanket chest, as I have said somewhere before, is my favourite piece ; but unfortunately I planned it with no particular relevance to blanket size, and whatever shape they were folded, they never quite fitted. If the full chest was left for half a minute they rose, like unbaked dough, and the humped mound oozed over the side. Once they were in, well thumped down, down banged the lid and click went the key.

Gradually the dairy became spotless, the kitchen emptier, and while Mat got breakfast I attacked what will some day prove my Waterloo—mattress packing. I know of no household article more difficult to pack than a mattress. It has no smallest inkling of its purpose in life; it struggles when one puts it on a bed ; it struggles when it is taken off. There is no pleasing it ; it lives in a state of perpetual discontent.

I threw myself on one end, trying to roll it up tightly. It resented this, and I had to kneel on it while I continued the rolling. To get the roll well started was the crucial part. Once that was done, and it was plain who was to be master I made it into a large Swiss roll, and then I adapted the instructions of the chain makers. " Lay the rope straight along the bed, and reverse the mattress on to it." I spread-eagled myself over it, and we reversed together rather than lose the hard-won, compact tightness of that roll, for given the slightest chance it attempted to swell all its muscles and, with a final convulsive kick, increased its girth by half, developing a large air space in the middle, so that it was too big to fit into the wardrobe.

Except for the damp and musty smell, the house was rapidly assuming the look it had on the day we arrived. Packages were piled on the hall seat, the kitchen was bare and echoing, and the glow in the grate was dying down to soft grey ash.

We hurried through the last jobs ; releasing the reservoir dam, locking the doors and dropping the keys to the bottom of the kit bag again, and, taking out the remaining baggage, we swung it over the fence to be put in the car. One final, sad look round, and we slammed the front door. The car lurched out of the shed, and at the sheep fold there was time for one backward farewell glance before the house dropped out of sight, and we sternly projected our minds ahead into Essex and drove on.

To end with departure seems to be the right kind of epilogue, for sometime at Blaen-y-cwm there will be a final Departure, and no future Arrival to anticipate.

The last few years have brought many changes to the valley ; among them, Kath and Iolo have left their long-house and moved to the next county ; our helpful neigh-bours at the Canol have gone down the valley, nearer to prosperity ; and the Canol has new owners, prepared to attempt a living in the mountains with fourteen pigs for us to look at as we pass, instead of the solitary of Isaf.

Sometime—may it be long deferred—there will be another change. We too shall move, not because any move we can make will bring us nearer to prosperity, but because, one day, in the constant struggle with the mountains and the elements, they will win—as they always do in the end.

For a time one can hold one's own, but they are too big and strong and relentless for it to be for more than a time. The empty houses falling to ruin in the cwms around are proof of that, and sooner or later, we too shall be added to the long list of those who have moved down the valley to a more sheltered existence.

When that day comes, and the door of Blaen-y-cwm closes, perhaps for another twenty years, perhaps for ever, although it will be a part of my life renounced, the going will be soft-ened by the knowledge that I shall never really leave that valley, and that the years spent among those rocks and mountains, cwms, lakes and woods are too deeply impressed in my memory ever to be forgotten. They are there for all time.